Table of Contents

2	Left vs. Right in Courts
6	Extreme Nationalism
9	Examples of Hard Right Movements
15	Examples of Hard Left Movements
17	Left & Right View Points
19	Left Wing Economics
22	Left Wing Social Policies
26	Left Wing in Government
29	Left Wing in Foreign Policy
33	Right Wing Economics
37	Right Wing Social Policies
42	Right Wing in Government
46	Right Wing Foreign Policy
50	Red vs. Blue – Political Topology
59	Liberal Left & Right – American Ideology
63	Left vs. Right Harming America
69	Defining a Centrist
74	Centrist Policies
83	Centrist Policies in Action
92	Woke (ism)
100	Woke in Politics
108	DEI
115	DEI in Personal Lives

In the context of the court system, "left" and "right" typically refer to political ideologies, but their influence on legal systems can be seen in how laws are interpreted and applied. Here's a breakdown of how the "left" and "right" might approach legal matters differently:

1. Interpretation of Laws

- **Right (Conservative):**
    - Tends to support a more originalist or textualist interpretation of the law, meaning that laws should be applied as they were originally written or as they were intended at the time of their passage.
    - May argue that judges should not create new laws through their rulings, but rather enforce the laws as they are.
- **Left (Liberal):**
    - More likely to support a living constitution or interpretive approach, where laws and their application evolve with societal changes.
    - This perspective might encourage judges to consider the broader social context and the consequences of their decisions, even if it involves interpreting laws in a more progressive way.
    -

2. Criminal Justice

- **Right (Conservative):**
    - Often favors harsher punishments, more focus on law and order, and a belief in the importance of deterrence in crime prevention.
    - Support for the death penalty and longer prison sentences for criminals.
- **Left (Liberal):**
    - Generally advocates for criminal justice reform, focusing on rehabilitation, restorative justice, and addressing systemic issues like racial inequality in the justice system.
    - Might oppose the death penalty and advocate for alternatives to incarceration for non-violent offenders.

3. Civil Rights and Liberties

- **Right (Conservative):**
    - Emphasizes the protection of individual freedoms, but might support limiting certain civil liberties (like in cases of national security or religious rights).
    - More likely to support policies that limit government intervention in personal matters.

- **Left (Liberal):**
    - **Advocates for expanded civil rights protections, often focusing on issues like LGBTQ+ rights, racial equality, and gender equality.**
    - **Supports government intervention in areas where individuals might be marginalized or discriminated against.**

4. Economic and Corporate Regulation

- **Right (Conservative):**
    - **Prefers limited regulation on businesses, favoring free market principles.**
    - **Tends to oppose excessive government oversight or regulation in economic matters.**
- **Left (Liberal):**
    - **Supports stronger regulatory policies to ensure fairness, protect workers, and prevent corporate abuses.**
    - **Advocates for policies like environmental protections, labor rights, and consumer protections that may require increased government involvement.**

5. Judicial Appointments

- **Right (Conservative):**

- **Typically prefers judges who are conservative in their approach, often looking for individuals who interpret laws strictly according to their original meaning or text.**

- Left (Liberal):
    - **Tends to favor judicial appointments that align with more progressive views, hoping to influence the court's rulings toward greater individual rights and liberties.**

These differences reflect broader political philosophies, and they can shape not just individual rulings but the overall direction of a legal system. However, in practice, judges are often expected to remain impartial and base their decisions on the law and facts of each case, regardless of political leanings.

Hard-right people, often referred to as **extreme right-wing** individuals or groups, hold beliefs that are more **rigid, conservative, and often radical** compared to mainstream right-wing ideology. While these views can vary depending on the country or context, **hard-right** ideologies are typically characterized by a **strong commitment to nationalism, authoritarianism, and traditionalism**, often combined with an **intolerance for progressive or liberal values**.

Here's a breakdown of the key features of hard-right beliefs:

1. Extreme Nationalism

- **Focus on National Superiority**: Hard-right individuals often place their own country or ethnic group above others, sometimes advocating for **ethnic or cultural homogeneity**.

- **Opposition to Immigration**: They tend to support **strict anti-immigration policies** and may promote **xenophobia** or **nativism**, believing that immigration threatens national identity and culture.

- **Patriotism & Sovereignty**: A strong belief in national sovereignty and rejecting international cooperation or influence from organizations like the United Nations or the European Union.

2. Authoritarianism

- **Support for Authoritarian Leaders**: Hard-right individuals often favor **strong, centralized leadership** and may endorse **dictatorship-like rule** if it maintains order and national unity.

- **Opposition to Political Freedom**: Some extreme-right groups may challenge democratic institutions, supporting **limited political freedoms**, such as restricting political opposition, media, or speech that doesn't align with their views.

- **Strict Law & Order**: Advocacy for strict law enforcement and harsh penalties for crime, often associated with support for **police militarization** and **surveillance**.

3. Traditionalism & Social Conservatism

- **Opposition to Social Progressivism**: Hard-right individuals often oppose changes related to **LGBTQ+ rights**, **gender equality**, and **reproductive rights** (e.g., abortion). They typically adhere to **traditional views on marriage**, family, and gender roles.

- **Religious Influence in Politics**: In some cases, hard-right ideologies are intertwined with **religious conservatism**, advocating for policies that reflect a particular faith (e.g., Christianity, Islam) in governance, schools, or public life.

- **Preservation of "Old Values"**: A strong belief in maintaining or returning to what they view as **traditional cultural, religious, or societal norms**, often resisting modernity and social change.

4. Anti-Communism & Anti-Leftism

- **Hostility Toward Left-Wing Politics**: Hard-right groups often have an intense aversion to socialist, communist, and progressive movements, viewing them as threats to the social order or capitalist economy.

- **Anti-Globalism**: A rejection of **globalism**, often coupled with **anti-establishment** sentiments, especially against international agreements or organizations that they see as undermining national interests.

5. Economic Views

- **Market-Oriented but Often Nationalist**: Hard-right ideologies often support **free-market capitalism**, but with a heavy focus on **economic nationalism** (e.g., protectionism, tariffs) to ensure that national industries thrive over foreign competition.

- **Anti-Welfare State**: Some hard-right groups oppose social welfare programs, viewing them as **state overreach** or enablers of dependency. They may believe that individuals should be responsible for their own economic success, and that government intervention is unnecessary or harmful.

6. Racism & Xenophobia

- **Ethnic Supremacy**: In extreme cases, hard-right ideologies may veer into **racism** or **white nationalism**, advocating for the dominance or preservation of a particular racial or ethnic group, often with an exclusionary stance toward minorities or immigrants.

- **Opposition to Multiculturalism**: Hard-right groups typically reject **multiculturalism** and **diversity**, believing in the superiority or exclusivity of their own culture or ethnicity.

Examples of Hard-Right Movements

- **Neo-Nazism and White Nationalism**: These groups hold extreme nationalist, racist, and anti-Semitic views and advocate for the **restoration of a "pure" national identity** through exclusionary policies.

- **Fascism**: A far-right ideology that includes **dictatorial power**, **forcible suppression of opposition**, and a focus on **nationalist militarism**. Historical examples include Mussolini's Italy and Nazi Germany.

- **Alt-Right (U.S.)**: A loosely connected group of individuals and movements that blend **white nationalism, anti-Semitism**, and opposition to progressive political correctness.

- **Nationalist Populism (e.g., some of Europe's far-right parties)**: Parties like **Jobbik** in Hungary or **Golden Dawn** in Greece promote strong nationalism, anti-immigration policies, and anti-European Union stances.

Summary of Hard-Right Beliefs

Hard-right individuals or groups generally support **authoritarian leadership, nationalism, anti-progressive** values, and **traditional social norms**. They may oppose social reforms on issues like gender, race, and immigration, and advocate for **rigid national identity** and **economic protectionism**. In extreme cases, their views may involve **xenophobia**, **racism**, or even **ethnic supremacist** ideologies.

Hard-left people, often referred to as **extreme left-wing** individuals or groups, hold more **radical and revolutionary** beliefs compared to mainstream left-wing ideologies. These views typically advocate for **fundamental change** to the political, economic, and social systems, often aiming to **upend existing structures** in pursuit of **equality, justice, and collective control**. While these views can vary, hard-left ideologies generally reject **capitalism** and advocate for more **socialist** or **communist** systems of governance.

Here's a breakdown of the key features of hard-left beliefs:

1. Anti-Capitalism & Socialist/Communist Ideals

- **Opposition to Capitalism**: Hard-left individuals reject capitalism, viewing it as inherently **exploitative** and leading to **inequality** and **class oppression**. They argue for the redistribution of wealth and power to the working class.

- **Support for Socialist/Communist Systems**: They advocate for **collective ownership** of the means of production, often calling for the nationalization of key industries (e.g., healthcare, transportation, energy) and the redistribution of resources.

- **Economic Equality**: Hard-left ideologies push for **wealth redistribution** through **progressive taxation**, universal welfare programs, and efforts to reduce the gap between the rich and poor.

2. Anti-Imperialism & Global Revolution

- **Opposition to Global Capitalism and Imperialism**: Hard-left groups tend to be critical of global institutions like the **IMF**, **World Bank**, and **WTO**, viewing them as instruments of **imperialist exploitation** that benefit wealthy nations at the expense of the Global South.

- **Revolutionary Change**: Many hard-left ideologies, especially those with **Marxist** or **Leninist** influences, advocate for **revolutionary movements** to overthrow capitalist governments and systems. They see this as a necessary step toward creating a **classless society**.

- **Solidarity with Global Struggles**: They often express solidarity with **revolutionary movements** or **resistance groups** in countries they perceive as being oppressed by capitalist powers or authoritarian regimes.

3. Class Struggle & Worker Empowerment

- **Class Consciousness**: Hard-left people focus on the **class struggle** between the working class (proletariat) and the capitalist class (bourgeoisie). They argue that true social change will only occur when the working class seizes power.

- **Worker Control**: They advocate for **direct democracy** in the workplace, including **worker cooperatives** and the collective management of industries. They envision a society where workers have control over their own labor and economic decisions.

---

4. Radical Social Change & Justice

- **Emphasis on Equality**: Hard-left ideologies advocate for **radical social reforms** to achieve equality in all aspects of life—gender, race, sexuality, and disability. They call for dismantling social hierarchies that contribute to **systemic oppression**.

- **Identity Politics**: Many hard-left groups focus on **intersectionality**, the idea that different forms of oppression (race, gender, class, etc.) are interconnected and must be addressed simultaneously.

- **Revolutionary Feminism**: Hard-left feminists advocate for a total restructuring of societal norms and systems that perpetuate gender inequality. This can involve rejecting traditional gender roles, advocating for **sex-positive policies**, and supporting **gender abolition**.

5. Environmentalism & Eco-Socialism

- **Eco-Socialism**: Many hard-left individuals embrace **eco-socialism**, which combines traditional socialist views with environmental justice. They argue that **capitalism** is inherently **unsustainable** and that the exploitation of natural resources must be replaced with **sustainable, collective economic systems**.

- **Climate Justice**: Hard-left movements often align with calls for **radical environmental action** to combat climate change. They may push for **socialized** or **publicly owned** green energy systems, rejecting **corporate** control of natural resources and energy markets.

6. Anti-Authoritarianism (In Some Cases)

- **Anarchism**: Some hard-left groups, particularly anarchists, reject all forms of state power, viewing the state as inherently coercive. They advocate for a **stateless, decentralized society** based on voluntary cooperation, direct democracy, and community self-management.

- **Direct Action**: Hard-left groups may support **direct action** tactics, such as protests, strikes, and **civil**

disobedience, to challenge the status quo and effect social change, often outside of traditional political systems.

- **Critique of State Socialism**: While some hard-left individuals may support socialist states, others are critical of historical examples like the Soviet Union, arguing that they became **authoritarian** and failed to create the type of democratic socialism they envision.

7. Radical Anti-Fascism & Anti-Racism

- **Anti-Fascism**: Hard-left individuals are often **anti-fascist** (Antifa), rejecting any form of **fascist** ideology, which they associate with **nationalism, racism**, and **authoritarianism**. They may take an active role in combating fascist movements or hate groups through both political resistance and direct action.

- **Opposition to Racism & Colonialism**: Hard-left groups are typically focused on **anti-racism**, pushing for **decolonization** and **reparations** for past wrongs, including slavery and indigenous displacement. They often advocate for the **empowerment of marginalized groups**, such as Black, Indigenous, and People of Color (BIPOC).

Examples of Hard-Left Movements

- **Marxism and Communism**: Groups or individuals who align with **Marxist** or **Leninist** thought, which aims for the overthrow of capitalism and the establishment of a **classless, stateless society**.

- **Anarchism**: A broad movement that seeks to abolish all forms of hierarchical authority, including the state, capitalism, and patriarchy.

- **Eco-Socialism**: Environmental movements that seek to address the climate crisis through socialist principles, aiming to reorganize society and the economy around sustainability rather than profit.

- **Antifa**: A loosely organized movement focused on direct action against far-right extremism, fascism, and racism, often through protests and counter-protests.

- **Workers' Councils and Syndicalism**: Movements that advocate for **direct worker control** over industries, rejecting traditional government-controlled socialism in favor of a more decentralized, democratic economic system.

Summary of Hard-Left Beliefs

Hard-left individuals or groups often push for **revolutionary change**, rejecting capitalism and advocating for **socialist** or **communist** societies where resources are collectively owned. They emphasize

equality, social justice, and **anti-imperialism**, seeking to challenge social hierarchies, colonial legacies, and environmental destruction. They may also engage in **direct action** to achieve these goals, often taking a more **radical, anti-authoritarian** approach than mainstream left-wing movements.

The political left and right are broad categories that describe different ideologies, values, and policy preferences. While these terms can vary in meaning across different countries and contexts, here are some general distinctions:

Left-Wing (Liberal, Progressive, Socialist in some cases)

- **Economic Policy**: Supports government intervention in the economy, higher taxes on the wealthy, social welfare programs, and stronger labor protections.

- **Social Issues**: Advocates for social justice, civil rights, and inclusivity (e.g., LGBTQ+ rights, racial equality, gender equality).

- **Government Role**: Favors a larger role for the government in regulating businesses, providing healthcare, education, and reducing economic inequality.

- **Foreign Policy**: More likely to support diplomacy, international cooperation, and restrictions on military interventions.

- **Examples**: Social democracy (e.g., Nordic countries), progressive policies in the U.S. (e.g., Bernie Sanders, Alexandria Ocasio-Cortez), Labour Party in the UK.

Right-Wing (Conservative, Libertarian, Nationalist in some cases)

- **Economic Policy**: Supports free-market capitalism, lower taxes, deregulation, and reduced government spending.
- **Social Issues**: Tends to emphasize tradition, national identity, and sometimes religious values; may oppose policies like affirmative action or expansive immigration.
- **Government Role**: Prefers a smaller government, emphasizing personal responsibility and private enterprise over state welfare programs.
- **Foreign Policy**: Can favor strong national defense, military interventions, and protectionist policies to prioritize domestic interests.
- **Examples**: U.S. Republican Party (e.g., Donald Trump, Ron DeSantis), UK Conservative Party, nationalist movements in Europe.

Caveats & Variations

- Some positions blur the lines (e.g., populist movements can mix left-wing economic policies with right-wing nationalism).
- Libertarians advocate for minimal government in both economic and social issues, which doesn't fit neatly into either category.
- Centrists or moderates adopt policies from both sides depending on the issue.

Left-wing economic policies generally emphasize **government intervention** in the economy to promote **economic equality, social welfare, and worker protections**. These policies often contrast with free-market, laissez-faire approaches favored by the right. Here are the key features of left-wing economic policies:

1. Wealth Redistribution

- **Progressive Taxation**: Higher tax rates on the wealthy and corporations to fund public services.
- **Welfare Programs**: Government-funded programs like unemployment benefits, food assistance, and housing support to reduce poverty.
- **Universal Basic Income (UBI)**: Some leftist policies propose direct cash payments to all citizens to reduce economic insecurity.

2. Strong Government Regulation

- **Minimum Wage Laws**: Ensuring a living wage to prevent worker exploitation.
- **Consumer Protection**: Laws regulating corporations to prevent fraud, monopolies, and unsafe products.
- **Environmental Regulations**: Policies like carbon taxes and green energy subsidies to combat climate change.

3. Public Services & Socialized Programs

- **Universal Healthcare**: Government-funded healthcare systems (e.g., NHS in the UK, Medicare-for-All proposals in the U.S.).
- **Free or Subsidized Education**: Expanding access to higher education and reducing student debt.
- **Public Transportation & Infrastructure Investment**: Large-scale government projects to improve roads, rail, and energy grids.

4. Labor Rights & Union Support

- **Stronger Unions**: Laws that protect labor unions and workers' rights to collective bargaining.
- **Paid Leave Policies**: Ensuring paid parental leave, sick leave, and vacation time.
- **Worker Co-Ops & Workplace Democracy**: Some leftist movements advocate for businesses being owned and operated by workers.

5. Government-Led Economic Growth

- **Public Jobs Programs**: Creating government jobs to reduce unemployment, especially in economic downturns (e.g., New Deal-style programs).
- **Industrial Policy**: Government support for certain industries (e.g., green energy, manufacturing) to steer economic growth.
- **Nationalization of Key Industries**: Some leftist policies support state ownership of essential sectors like healthcare, energy, or transportation.

Examples of Left-Wing Economic Models

- **Nordic Model (Scandinavian Countries)**: High taxes, strong welfare state, and a mix of free-market capitalism and government intervention.

- **New Deal (U.S., 1930s)**: Massive government spending and social programs to address economic inequality.

- **Democratic Socialism (Bernie Sanders, Jeremy Corbyn)**: Market economy with heavy government regulation and strong social safety nets.

- **Full Socialism (Cuba, Venezuela, former USSR)**: State control of most industries, though with mixed economic success.

Left-wing social policies generally emphasize **progressive change, equality, and government action** to address societal inequalities. These policies often focus on civil rights, social justice, and inclusivity. Here are some key left-wing positions on social issues:

1. Civil Rights & Social Justice

- **Racial Equality**: Supports policies like affirmative action, anti-discrimination laws, and police reform to address systemic racism.

- **LGBTQ+ Rights**: Advocates for same-sex marriage, anti-discrimination protections, gender-affirming healthcare, and LGBTQ+ representation.

- **Gender Equality**: Pushes for equal pay, reproductive rights, and policies to address workplace discrimination.

2. Immigration & Multiculturalism

- **Pro-Immigration Policies**: Advocates for pathways to citizenship, refugee protections, and opposition to strict border enforcement.

- **Multiculturalism**: Supports diverse cultural representation and policies that protect minority groups' rights.

3. Criminal Justice Reform

- **Opposition to Mass Incarceration**: Seeks to reduce prison populations, decriminalize minor offenses (e.g., drug possession), and promote rehabilitation over punishment.

- **Police Reform**: Calls for increased accountability, demilitarization, and alternative community safety programs.

- **Abolitionist Movements**: Some on the far-left advocate for abolishing prisons and replacing them with restorative justice systems.

4. Healthcare & Reproductive Rights

- **Universal Healthcare**: Supports government-funded healthcare to ensure access for all.

- **Abortion Rights**: Advocates for legal and accessible abortion, opposing restrictions like bans or waiting periods.

- **Mental Health Services**: Pushes for increased government funding for mental health and addiction treatment programs.

5. Education & Free Speech

- **Free or Subsidized Higher Education**: Supports tuition-free college and student debt forgiveness.

- **Anti-Censorship (in Some Contexts)**: Advocates against book bans and for free speech protections, especially for marginalized groups.

- **Diversity & Inclusion in Education**: Encourages inclusive curriculums, such as ethnic studies, LGBTQ+ history, and anti-racist education.

6. Environmental Justice

- **Climate Change Action**: Supports policies like the Green New Deal, carbon taxes, and government investment in renewable energy.

- **Environmental Protections**: Advocates for stricter regulations on corporations to reduce pollution and preserve natural resources.

- **Indigenous Land & Water Rights**: Supports protecting Indigenous sovereignty and land from corporate exploitation.

7. Gun Control

- **Stricter Gun Laws**: Supports universal background checks, assault weapon bans, and red flag laws to prevent gun violence.

- **Public Safety Over Gun Rights**: Prioritizes collective safety over individual gun ownership rights.

8. Workers' Rights & Economic Justice

- **Strong Labor Protections**: Supports higher minimum wages, paid family leave, and union protections.

- **Universal Basic Income (UBI)**: Some leftists advocate for a guaranteed income to reduce economic inequality.

Examples of Left-Wing Social Policies in Action

- **Civil Rights Movement (1960s, U.S.)**: Fought for racial and voting rights.

- **Marriage Equality (2010s, U.S./Europe)**: Legalized same-sex marriage in many countries.

- **Green New Deal (Proposed, U.S.)**: Aims to tackle climate change through government investment in renewable energy.

- **Nordic Social Model**: Combines progressive social policies with a strong welfare state.

Left-wing politics generally advocate for a **larger and more active government** that plays a key role in regulating the economy, providing public services, and addressing social inequalities. Here's how left-wing ideologies typically define the government's role:

1. Economic Regulation & Wealth Redistribution

- **Progressive Taxation**: Higher taxes on corporations and the wealthy to fund public services and social programs.

- **Market Regulation**: Government oversight to prevent corporate monopolies, protect consumers, and ensure fair wages.

- **Public Ownership**: Some leftist policies advocate for government control or heavy regulation of key industries like healthcare, energy, and transportation.

2. Social Welfare & Public Services

- **Universal Healthcare**: Government-funded healthcare systems (e.g., Medicare-for-All, NHS in the UK).

- **Education Access**: Free or subsidized higher education, student loan forgiveness, and public investment in schools.

- **Housing & Basic Needs**: Programs like public housing, rent control, and food assistance to reduce poverty.

3. Civil Rights & Social Justice

- **Legal Protections**: Anti-discrimination laws, affirmative action, and voting rights protections.
- **Criminal Justice Reform**: Government intervention to reduce mass incarceration, reform policing, and provide rehabilitation services.
- **LGBTQ+ & Gender Rights**: Laws ensuring marriage equality, workplace protections, and reproductive rights.

4. Environmental Protection

- **Climate Change Action**: Government-led investment in renewable energy, carbon taxes, and environmental regulations.
- **Green New Deal-Style Policies**: Large-scale public projects to transition to a sustainable economy.

5. Labor Rights & Workplace Protections

- **Support for Unions**: Laws strengthening collective bargaining and preventing union-busting.
- **Workplace Regulations**: Minimum wage laws, paid leave, and workplace safety standards.

6. Infrastructure & Public Investment

- **Government-Led Development**: Public transportation, broadband expansion, and job programs.
- **Public Jobs Programs**: Direct government employment initiatives (e.g., FDR's New Deal programs).

7. National & Global Policy

- **Diplomatic Foreign Policy**: Emphasis on international cooperation, diplomacy, and human rights rather than military intervention.

- **Immigration Rights**: Pathways to citizenship, refugee protections, and opposition to strict border enforcement policies.

Left-wing foreign policies generally emphasize **diplomacy, international cooperation, human rights, and anti-militarism** over aggressive interventionism or unilateralism. While policies vary depending on the country and political movement, here are the key themes of left-wing foreign policy:

1. Diplomacy & Multilateralism

- **Stronger International Cooperation**: Supports working with global organizations like the United Nations (UN), World Health Organization (WHO), and regional alliances (e.g., European Union, African Union).

- **Emphasis on Diplomacy Over Military Action**: Prefers negotiations and peace-building efforts over military intervention.

- **Support for Treaties & Agreements**: Advocates for arms control agreements, climate accords (e.g., Paris Agreement), and international trade deals that prioritize labor and environmental protections.

2. Human Rights & Social Justice

- **Humanitarian Aid & Refugee Protections**: Encourages assistance for displaced populations and asylum seekers.

- **Opposition to Authoritarian Regimes**: Condemns human rights violations but favors diplomatic pressure over military intervention.

- **Fair Trade Policies**: Supports trade agreements that prioritize workers' rights, environmental standards, and fair wages rather than corporate profits.

3. Anti-Imperialism & Non-Interventionism

- **Opposition to Military Intervention**: Criticizes foreign wars and regime-change operations (e.g., Iraq War, Vietnam War).
- **Decolonization & Reparations**: Some leftist movements advocate for addressing colonial legacies through reparations or economic assistance.
- **Reduction of Military Spending**: Prefers redirecting defense budgets toward domestic social programs, infrastructure, and climate initiatives.

4. Climate Change & Global Sustainability

- **Global Green Policies**: Supports international climate agreements, funding for renewable energy in developing nations, and corporate accountability for environmental harm.
- **Regulation of Global Corporations**: Seeks to hold multinational companies accountable for labor abuses, tax evasion, and environmental destruction.

5. Immigration & Refugee Rights

- **Pathways to Citizenship**: Supports humane immigration policies, asylum protections, and opposition to strict border enforcement.
- **Ending Harsh Detention Practices**: Advocates for humane treatment of migrants and alternatives to detention centers.

6. Demilitarization & Arms Control

- **Nuclear Disarmament**: Supports arms reduction treaties and efforts to eliminate nuclear weapons.
- **Reducing Military Industrial Influence**: Criticizes the influence of defense contractors and arms manufacturers in shaping foreign policy.
- **Cutting Foreign Military Aid to Authoritarian Regimes**: Calls for ending arms sales to governments accused of human rights violations.

Examples of Left-Wing Foreign Policy in Action

- **Paris Climate Agreement (2015)**: A global commitment to reduce carbon emissions, supported by left-wing governments.
- **Iraq War Opposition (2003)**: Many left-leaning politicians and activists opposed U.S. military intervention in Iraq.
- **Nordic Model Diplomacy**: Scandinavian countries often lead in peace mediation, foreign aid, and climate policies.

- **Support for Palestinian Statehood**: Many leftist movements advocate for Palestinian rights and a two-state solution.

Summary

Left-wing foreign policy is generally **anti-war, pro-diplomacy, focused on human rights, and committed to climate action**. It opposes military interventionism, seeks fair economic relations, and prioritizes humanitarian efforts over corporate or nationalistic interests.

Right-wing economic policies generally emphasize **free markets, low taxes, minimal government intervention, and individual responsibility** over wealth redistribution and social welfare programs. Here are the key aspects of right-wing economic policies:

1. Free-Market Capitalism

- **Limited Government Intervention**: Advocates for minimal regulation of businesses to encourage economic growth and innovation.

- **Privatization**: Supports transferring public services (e.g., healthcare, education, transportation) from government control to private companies.

- **Deregulation**: Seeks to reduce government rules on businesses, especially in finance, energy, and labor markets.

2. Lower Taxes & Fiscal Conservatism

- **Low Corporate & Income Taxes**: Believes lower taxes encourage business investment and job creation.

- **Flat Taxes or Simplified Tax Codes**: Some right-wing policies propose a single tax rate for all income levels rather than progressive taxation.

- **Reduced Government Spending**: Opposes large social welfare programs, focusing instead on budget cuts and deficit reduction.

3. Limited Welfare & Social Programs

- **Smaller Social Safety Nets**: Prefers private charities and individual responsibility over government-funded welfare programs.
- **Work Requirements for Benefits**: Often supports requiring employment or job training for those receiving government assistance.
- **Opposition to Universal Healthcare**: Prefers private healthcare systems over government-run models.

4. Pro-Business & Investment Policies

- **Corporate Tax Cuts & Incentives**: Encourages investment and job creation by reducing business taxes.
- **Right-to-Work Laws**: Limits the power of labor unions, making union membership optional in workplaces.
- **Encouraging Entrepreneurship**: Favors policies that reduce barriers to starting and running a business.

5. Trade & Globalization

- **Free Trade Agreements**: Supports global trade with minimal tariffs and restrictions (though some right-wing populists favor protectionism).

- **Deregulated Markets**: Prefers fewer restrictions on international trade, capital flow, and multinational corporations.
- **Tax Incentives for Domestic Manufacturing**: Some right-wing policies promote tax breaks to keep jobs within the country.

6. Reduced Government Debt & Balanced Budgets

- **Spending Cuts Over Tax Increases**: Seeks to reduce national debt by cutting spending rather than raising taxes.
- **Privatizing Government Services**: Advocates for outsourcing public services to private companies to cut costs.

7. Property Rights & Opposition to Wealth Redistribution

- **Strong Private Property Protections**: Opposes government seizure or heavy taxation of private assets.
- **Criticism of Socialism & Redistribution**: Argues that wealth should be earned through effort rather than redistributed by the government.

Examples of Right-Wing Economic Policies in Action

- **Reaganomics (U.S., 1980s)**: Tax cuts, deregulation, and reduced government spending.
- **Thatcherism (UK, 1980s)**: Privatization of state-owned industries and weakening of labor unions.

- **Trump Tax Cuts (U.S., 2017)**: Major corporate tax cuts and deregulation efforts.
- **Singapore's Economic Model**: Low taxes, minimal regulation, and pro-business policies with a strong focus on individual responsibility.

Summary

Right-wing economic policies prioritize **low taxes, free-market capitalism, deregulation, and limited government involvement in social welfare**. These policies argue that economic growth is best achieved when businesses and individuals have more control over their finances, rather than relying on government redistribution.

Right-wing social policies generally emphasize **tradition, national identity, individual responsibility, and limited government intervention in cultural and social matters**. While policies can vary by country and political movement, here are the key aspects of right-wing social issues:

1. Traditional Values & Social Conservatism

- **Opposition to Progressive Social Changes**: Advocates for preserving traditional family structures and cultural values.

- **Religious Influence in Society**: Supports religious freedoms and, in some cases, policies that reflect religious beliefs (e.g., opposition to abortion or same-sex marriage).

- **Support for Traditional Gender Roles**: Some right-wing movements emphasize traditional male and female roles in family and society.

2. Law & Order

- **Tough on Crime Policies**: Supports strict sentencing laws, including the death penalty and mandatory minimums.

- **Strong Policing & Border Security**: Advocates for increased funding for law enforcement and harsher penalties for criminal activity.

- **Opposition to Drug Legalization**: Generally against the decriminalization of drugs, favoring strict enforcement instead.

3. Nationalism & Immigration Control

- **Strict Immigration Laws**: Supports strong border enforcement, deportation of illegal immigrants, and limiting asylum policies.

- **National Identity & Patriotism**: Encourages national pride, historical preservation, and policies that prioritize native-born citizens.

- **Opposition to Multiculturalism**: Some right-wing groups believe in cultural assimilation rather than maintaining diverse cultural identities.

4. Gun Rights & Self-Defense

- **Support for Gun Ownership**: Advocates for the right to bear arms, often opposing gun control measures.

- **Self-Defense Laws**: Supports "Stand Your Ground" laws and other policies that allow individuals to protect themselves with firearms.

5. Opposition to Expansive LGBTQ+ Rights

- **Traditional Definition of Marriage**: Opposes same-sex marriage in favor of traditional male-female unions.

- **Restrictions on Gender-Affirming Care**: Supports limiting or banning hormone treatments and surgeries for transgender individuals, particularly minors.

- **Limits on LGBTQ+ Education & Representation**: Some right-wing groups push against LGBTQ+ content in schools and media.

6. Opposition to Political Correctness & "Woke" Culture

- **Free Speech Advocacy**: Opposes speech restrictions, "cancel culture," and diversity mandates in workplaces and schools.
- **Resistance to DEI (Diversity, Equity, Inclusion) Programs**: Argues that these initiatives promote unfair advantages rather than true equality.

7. Education & Parental Rights

- **School Choice & Vouchers**: Supports alternatives to public education, such as private, religious, or homeschooling options.
- **Opposition to Progressive Curriculum**: Rejects Critical Race Theory (CRT), gender identity education, and left-wing historical narratives in schools.
- **Parental Rights in Education**: Advocates for greater parental control over what children learn in school, including the ability to opt out of certain topics.

8. Anti-Abortion & Pro-Life Policies

- **Opposition to Abortion**: Supports banning or restricting abortion, often based on religious or moral beliefs.

- **Promotion of Adoption & Family Values**: Encourages alternatives to abortion, such as adoption and financial support for pregnant women.

9. Environmental Policy Skepticism

- **Opposition to Climate Regulations**: Criticizes strict environmental policies that could harm businesses and jobs.

- **Support for Fossil Fuels**: Advocates for energy independence through oil, coal, and natural gas rather than government-mandated green energy policies.

Examples of Right-Wing Social Policies in Action

- **Tough-on-Crime Laws (U.S.)**: Mandatory sentencing policies and increased police funding.

- **Brexit (UK, 2016)**: A nationalist movement focused on sovereignty and stricter immigration policies.

- **Florida's Education Laws (2022-Present)**: Limits on LGBTQ+ discussions in schools, bans on CRT, and increased parental rights in education.

- **Abortion Bans in Conservative U.S. States**: Restrictions or complete bans on abortion following the reversal of Roe v. Wade.

Summary

Right-wing social policies typically **prioritize tradition, law and order, national identity, and limited government interference in cultural issues**. These policies often resist rapid social change, emphasizing **personal responsibility, religious values, and national sovereignty** over progressive social justice movements.

Right-wing politics generally advocate for a **limited government** that focuses on national security, law and order, and protecting individual freedoms, while minimizing government intervention in the economy and social programs. Here's a breakdown of how right-wing ideologies typically define the role of government:

---

1. Limited Government & Individual Responsibility

- **Small Government Approach**: Prefers minimal government intervention in business, personal lives, and economic affairs.

- **Emphasis on Personal Responsibility**: Believes individuals and private institutions, rather than the government, should solve social and economic problems.

- **Decentralization of Power**: Supports state or local control over policies rather than centralized federal control.

---

2. Free-Market Economy & Deregulation

- **Minimal Economic Regulation**: Reduces government oversight of businesses to encourage economic growth.

- **Lower Taxes**: Advocates for tax cuts to boost private sector investment and individual wealth.

- **Privatization of Public Services**: Supports shifting services like healthcare, education, and transportation from government to private sector control.

3. Law & Order

- **Strong National Security & Border Control**: Emphasizes strict immigration policies and a well-funded military.

- **Tough-on-Crime Policies**: Advocates for strong law enforcement, harsh penalties for crime, and the death penalty.

- **Protection of Gun Rights**: Supports the right to bear arms as a means of self-defense and protection against government overreach.

4. Traditional Social Values

- **Government Should Protect Cultural & Religious Values**: Some right-wing movements believe the government should uphold traditional family structures and moral values.

- **Opposition to Expansive Social Programs**: Believes social welfare can lead to dependency and should be limited.

5. Foreign Policy: National Interest First

- **Strong National Sovereignty**: Opposes global governance structures that could undermine national control.

- **America First/Economic Nationalism**: Prioritizes domestic industries over international trade agreements.

- **Military Strength & Interventionism (in Some Cases)**: Some right-wing ideologies support a strong military presence abroad to protect national interests.

6. Fiscal Conservatism & Balanced Budgets

- **Spending Cuts Over Tax Increases**: Advocates reducing government spending rather than increasing taxes to balance budgets.

- **Opposition to Debt-Driven Welfare Programs**: Believes government should not take on excessive debt for social spending.

Examples of Right-Wing Government Policies in Action

- **Reaganomics (U.S., 1980s)**: Tax cuts, deregulation, and reduced government programs.

- **Thatcherism (UK, 1980s)**: Privatization of state-owned industries and reduced union influence.

- **Conservative Immigration Policies (U.S., UK, Australia)**: Stricter border enforcement and merit-based immigration systems.

- **Gun Rights Laws (U.S.)**: Opposition to federal gun control laws in favor of state and individual rights.

Summary

Right-wing government philosophy generally supports **limited government, free-market economics, strong national security, and traditional values**, with an emphasis on **personal responsibility over government dependency**.

Right-wing foreign policies generally emphasize **national sovereignty, military strength, economic nationalism, and a skeptical approach to globalism**. While policies vary among different conservative movements, here are the key themes of right-wing foreign policy:

1. Nationalism & Sovereignty First

- **Opposition to Globalism**: Skeptical of international organizations (e.g., United Nations, World Economic Forum) that could undermine national independence.

- **America First / National Interest First**: Prioritizes domestic industries, workers, and security over international commitments.

- **Strict Immigration Policies**: Supports tighter border control, merit-based immigration, and opposition to refugee resettlement programs.

2. Strong Military & Defense Policy

- **Increased Military Spending**: Advocates for a well-funded military to maintain global power and deterrence.

- **Peace Through Strength**: Supports military alliances (e.g., NATO) but favors showing force over diplomacy in conflicts.

- **Willingness to Use Military Force**: More open to preemptive strikes and unilateral interventions to protect national interests.

3. Economic Nationalism & Trade Policy

- **Opposition to Free Trade Agreements (in Some Cases)**: Right-wing populists often criticize trade deals that they believe hurt domestic jobs (e.g., opposition to NAFTA, USMCA renegotiation).

- **Tariffs & Protectionism**: Supports tariffs on foreign goods to boost domestic manufacturing and reduce reliance on imports.

- **Energy Independence**: Advocates for using domestic oil, coal, and gas rather than relying on international energy markets.

4. Skepticism of Foreign Aid & Global Institutions

- **Reduced Foreign Aid**: Prefers cutting international aid unless it directly benefits national security or economic interests.

- **Opposition to Climate Agreements**: Many right-wing policies reject treaties like the Paris Climate Accord, arguing they harm economic growth.

- **Limited Involvement in International Governance**: Critical of organizations like the UN,

EU, and WHO that impose regulations on national policies.

5. Strong Alliances with Like-Minded Nations

- **Preference for Bilateral Agreements**: Rather than multilateral agreements, right-wing foreign policy often seeks one-on-one deals that benefit national interests.

- **Support for Israel**: Many right-wing governments strongly support Israel due to strategic, religious, and ideological reasons.

- **Opposition to Communist & Authoritarian Regimes**: Often takes a hardline stance against China, North Korea, Cuba, and Venezuela.

6. Hardline Stance on Terrorism & Security Threats

- **Aggressive Counterterrorism Policies**: Supports military intervention and surveillance programs to prevent terrorist threats.

- **Opposition to Nuclear Agreements with Adversaries**: Prefers strict sanctions and deterrence over diplomacy with nations like Iran and North Korea.

-

Examples of Right-Wing Foreign Policy in Action

- **Trump's America First Doctrine (2016-2020)**: Tariffs on China, withdrawal from global agreements, border security policies.

- **Brexit (UK, 2016-Present)**: Conservative-led movement to leave the EU for greater national sovereignty.

- **Israel Support Policies (U.S. & UK, various leaders)**: Recognizing Jerusalem as Israel's capital, increased military aid.

- **Cold War Strategies (U.S., 1947-1991)**: Anti-communist foreign policy, military interventions, and alliances against the Soviet Union.

Summary

Right-wing foreign policy generally emphasizes **national sovereignty, military strength, economic self-reliance, and skepticism of international institutions**. It prioritizes **security, defense, and trade policies that benefit the nation first**, often taking a **hardline stance against adversaries and illegal immigration**.

Beyond Red vs. Blue: The Political Typology

Even in a polarized era, deep divisions in both partisan coalitions

How we did this

Partisan polarization remains the dominant, seemingly unalterable condition of American politics. Republicans and Democrats agree on very little – and when they do, it often is in the shared belief that they have little in common.

The 2021 political typology

% of ____ who are ...

	General public	Rep/Lean Rep	Dem/Lean Dem
Faith and Flag Conservatives	10	23	6
Committed Conservatives	7		13
Populist Right	11	15	16
Ambivalent Right	12		
Stressed Sideliners	15	23	28
Outsider Left	10		
Democratic Mainstays	16	18	23
Establishment Liberals	13	15	12
Progressive Left	6		

Source: Survey of U.S. adults conducted July 8-18, 2021.

PEW RESEARCH CENTER

Yet the gulf that separates Republicans and Democrats sometimes obscures the divisions and diversity of views that exist within both partisan coalitions – and the fact that many Americans do not fit easily into either one.

Republicans are divided on some principles long associated with the GOP: an affinity for businesses and corporations, support for low taxes and opposition to abortion. Democrats face substantial internal differences as well – some that are long-standing, such as on the importance of religion in society, others more recent. For example, while Democrats widely share the goal of combating racial inequality in the United States, they differ on whether systemic change is required to achieve that goal.

These intraparty disagreements present multiple challenges for both parties: They complicate the already difficult task of governing in a divided nation. In addition, to succeed politically, the parties must maintain the loyalty of highly politically engaged, more ideological voters, while also attracting support among less engaged voters – many of them younger – with weaker partisan ties.

Pew Research Center's new political typology provides a road map to today's fractured political landscape. It segments the public into nine distinct groups, based on an analysis of their attitudes and values. The study is primarily based on a survey of 10,221 adults conducted July 8-18, 2021; it also draws from several additional interviews with these respondents conducted since January 2020.

This is the Center's eighth political typology since 1987, but it differs from earlier such studies in several important ways. It is the first typology conducted on Pew Research Center's nationally representative American Trends Panel, which provides the benefit of a large sample size and the ability to include a wealth of other political data for the analysis, including the Center's validated voter study.

The four Democratic-oriented typology groups highlight the party's racial and ethnic diversity, as well as the unwieldy nature of the current Democratic coalition

They include two very different groups of liberal Democrats: **Progressive Left** and **Establishment Liberals**. Progressive Left, the only majority White, non-Hispanic group of Democrats, have very liberal views on virtually every issue and support far-reaching changes to address racial injustice and expand the social safety net. Establishment Liberals, while just as liberal in many ways as Progressive Left, are far less persuaded of the need for sweeping change.

Two other Democratic-aligned groups could not be more different from each other, both demographically and in their relationship to the party. **Democratic Mainstays**, the largest Democratic-oriented group, as well as the oldest on average, are unshakeable Democratic loyalists and have a moderate tilt on some issues. **Outsider Left**, the youngest typology group, voted overwhelmingly for Joe Biden a year ago and are very liberal in most of their views, but they are deeply frustrated with the political system – including the Democratic Party and its leaders.

The four Republican-oriented groups include three groups of conservatives: **Faith and Flag Conservatives** are intensely conservative in all realms; they are far more likely than all other typology groups to say government policies should support religious values and that compromise in politics is just "selling out on what you believe in." **Committed Conservatives** also express conservative views across the board, but with a somewhat softer edge, particularly on issues of immigration and America's place in the world. **Populist Right**, who have less formal education than most other typology groups and are among the most likely to live in rural areas, are highly critical of both immigrants and major U.S. corporations.

Ambivalent Right, the youngest and least conservative GOP-aligned group, hold conservative views about the size of government, the economic system and issues of race and gender. But they are the only group on the political right in which majorities favor legal abortion and say marijuana should be legal for recreational and medical use. They are also distinct in their views about Donald Trump – while a majority voted for him in 2020, most say they would prefer he not continue to be a major political figure.

The only typology group without a clear partisan orientation – **Stressed Sideliners** – also is the group with the lowest level of political engagement. Stressed Sideliners, who make up 15% of the public but constituted just 10% of voters in 2020, have a mix of conservative and liberal views but are largely defined by their minimal interest in politics.

Here are the main findings from the new political typology:

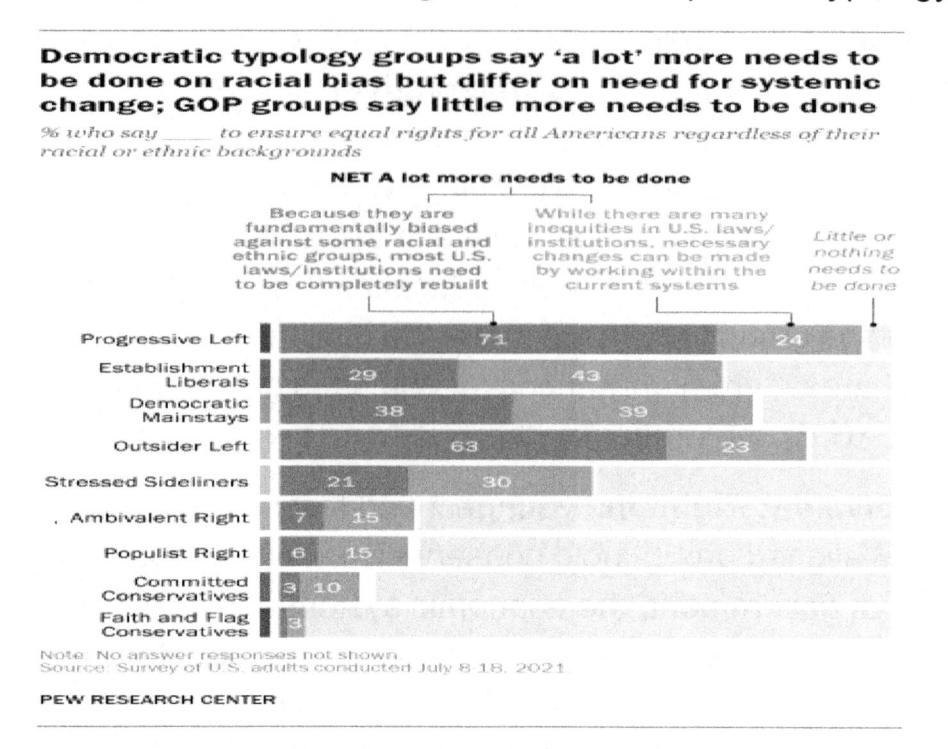

Democratic typology groups say 'a lot' more needs to be done on racial bias but differ on need for systemic change; GOP groups say little more needs to be done

% who say ____ to ensure equal rights for all Americans regardless of their racial or ethnic backgrounds

NET A lot more needs to be done

	Because they are fundamentally biased against some racial and ethnic groups, most U.S. laws/institutions need to be completely rebuilt	While there are many inequities in U.S. laws/institutions, necessary changes can be made by working within the current systems	Little or nothing needs to be done
Progressive Left	71		24
Establishment Liberals	29	43	
Democratic Mainstays	38	39	
Outsider Left	63		23
Stressed Sideliners	21	30	
Ambivalent Right	7	15	
Populist Right	6	15	
Committed Conservatives	3	10	
Faith and Flag Conservatives		3	

Note: No answer responses not shown.
Source: Survey of U.S. adults conducted July 8-18, 2021.

PEW RESEARCH CENTER

Racial injustice remains a dividing line in U.S. politics. Perhaps no issue is more divisive than racial injustice in the U.S. Among the four Republican-oriented typology groups, no more than about a quarter say a lot more needs to be done to ensure equal rights for all Americans regardless of their racial or ethnic background; by comparison, no fewer than about three-quarters of any Democratic group say a lot more needs to be done to achieve this goal. However, Democrats differ over whether the changes to ensure equal rights for all can be achieved by working within the current system, or whether most laws and institutions need to be completely rebuilt. Progressive Left and Outsider Left are far more likely than the two other Democratic groups to say systemic change is needed to combat racial bias.

Democrats prefer bigger government – but how big? There are much bigger divides *between* parties than *within* them on opinions about the size of government. Democratic-aligned groups overwhelmingly prefer a bigger government providing more services; GOP groups, by similar margins, favor smaller government. But when asked if government services should be *greatly* expanded from current levels, Democrats are divided: A clear majority of Progressive Left (63%) favor greatly expanding government services, compared with about a third in other Democratic-oriented groups.

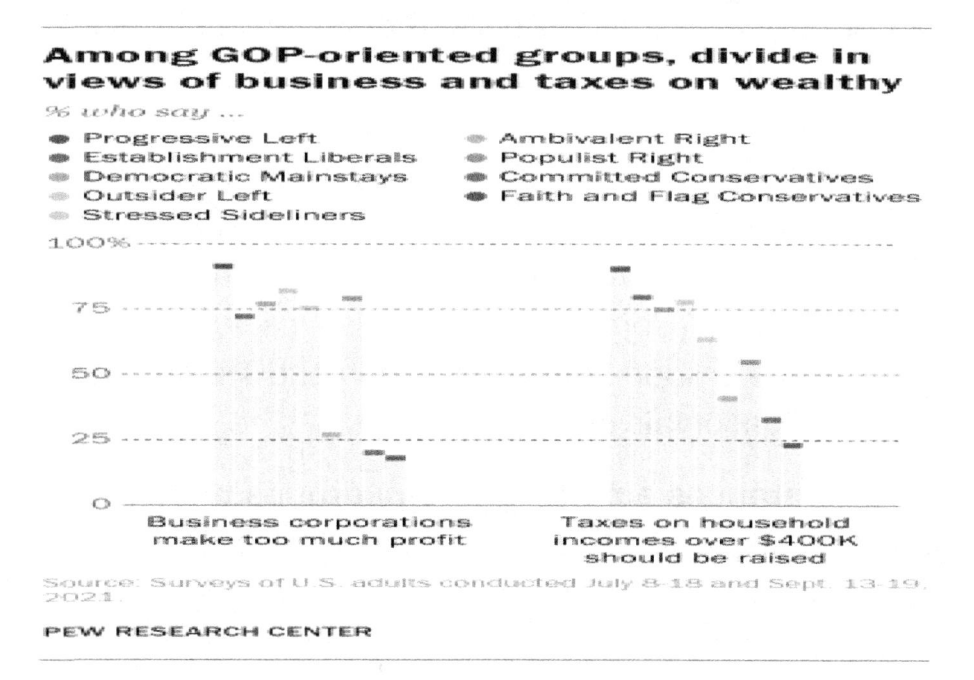

Among GOP-oriented groups, divide in views of business and taxes on wealthy

% who say ...

- Progressive Left
- Establishment Liberals
- Democratic Mainstays
- Outsider Left
- Stressed Sideliners
- Ambivalent Right
- Populist Right
- Committed Conservatives
- Faith and Flag Conservatives

Business corporations make too much profit

Taxes on household incomes over $400K should be raised

Source: Surveys of U.S. adults conducted July 8-18 and Sept. 13-19, 2021.

PEW RESEARCH CENTER

Economic policy – including taxes – divides the GOP. As noted, Populist Right diverge sharply from traditional GOP positions with their very negative views of corporations; just 17% say most corporations make a fair profit, which places this conservative group much closer to Democratic groups than to their Republican counterparts. And a majority of Populist Right (56%) favor raising taxes on household incomes above $400,000, as do 42% of Ambivalent Right (and substantial majorities in all Democratic-aligned groups).

Republicans' complicated views of Trump. The Republican-oriented typology groups each supported Trump by wide margins in 2020. Yet the survey shows substantial differences among GOP groups over Trump's future political role. In two of the four groups – Faith and Flag Conservatives and Populist Right – majorities want Trump to remain a major political figure *and* run for president again in 2024. And only among Populist Right does a clear plurality view Trump as the best president of the past 40 years. Among other Republican-aligned groups, more either view Ronald Reagan as the best recent president (Committed Conservatives, Ambivalent Right), or are divided between Reagan and Trump (Faith and Flag Conservatives).

Stark differences among typology groups on U.S. global standing. When asked whether the U.S. is superior to all other countries, it is among the greatest countries, or there are other countries that are better, there is relative agreement across six of nine typology groups: About half or more in this very ideologically mixed set of groups – including Establishment Liberals and Populist Right – say the U.S. is *among* the greatest countries in the world. Faith and Flag Conservatives are the only group in which a majority (69%) says the U.S. *stands above* all other countries. Conversely, Progressive Left (75%) and Outsider Left (63%) are the only typology groups in which majorities say there are other countries *better than* the U.S.

Groups in the ideological middle show lower levels of engagement with politics

% who say they follow what's going on in government and public affairs most of the time

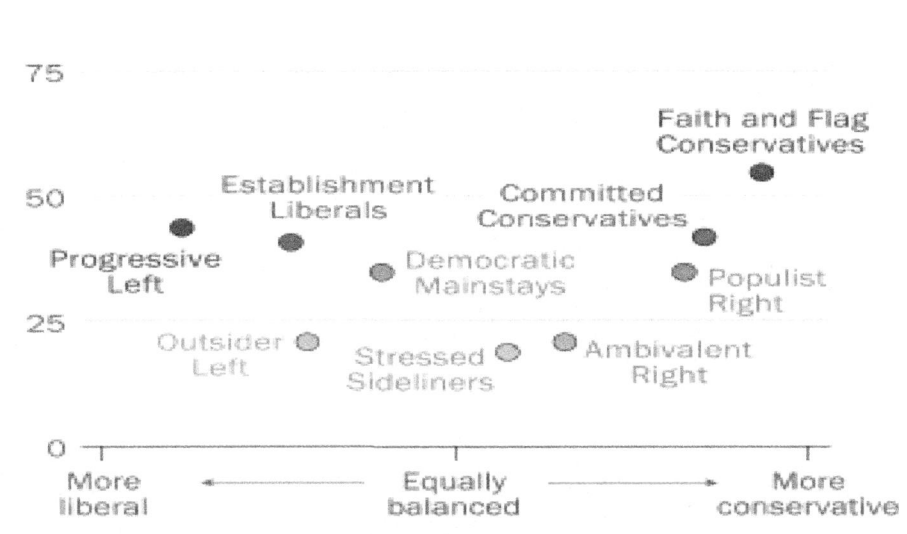

PEW RESEARCH CENTER

Is there a 'middle' in politics today? Surveys by Pew Research Center and other national polling organizations have found broad support, in principle, for a third major political party. Yet the typology study finds that the three groups with the largest shares of self-identified independents (most of whom lean toward a party) – Stressed Sideliners, Outsider Left and Ambivalent Right – have very little in common politically. Stressed Sideliners hold mixed views; Ambivalent Right are conservative on many economic issues, while moderate on some social issues; and Outsider Left are very liberal on most issues, especially on race and the social safety net. What these groups do have in common is relatively low interest in politics: They had the lowest rates of voting in the 2020 presidential election and are less likely than other groups to follow government and public affairs most of the time.

'Liberal', 'left,' 'conservative,' and 'right': Americans identify their ideology

When pollsters at YouGov want to show how American views on an issue differ across the political spectrum, we frequently break out respondents by their responses to a question about ideology — are they "liberal," "moderate," or "conservative"?

But these commonly used ideological labels don't sit well with some people. For example, while the term "liberal" is often used in the U.S. as a synonym for left-of-center, it also has different definitions that can exclude some people on the left and include some people on the right.

YouGov asked Americans to place their political views on a scale from "very liberal" to "very conservative" — and also on a scale from "far left" to "far right."

Overall, around 26% of Americans describe themselves as "liberal" or "very liberal," and another 32% describe themselves as "moderate." 33% describe themselves as "conservative" or "very conservative."

That roughly matches up with where Americans place themselves on a left-right spectrum. 27% of U.S. adult citizens say their politics are "far left," "left," or "center-left," while 24% say their politics are "center," and 34% say they're "far right," "right," or "center-right."

Americans' self-placement on the liberal-conservative spectrum roughly lines up with how they place themselves on the left-right spectrum, but there are some exceptions. 55% of the "very liberal" describe themselves as "far left," similar to the 46% of the "very conservative" who say they're "far right" and the 55% of moderates who say they're in the "center."

Americans who describe themselves as "liberal" are more likely to say their political viewpoint is "left" or "center-left" than are those who call themselves "very liberal." Likewise, those who say they're "conservative" are more likely to say they're "right" or "center-right" than are those who call themselves "very conservative."

Only 5% of those who say they're "liberal" (but not "very liberal") call themselves "far left," and only 3% of those who say they're "conservative" (but not "very conservative") say they're "far right."

71% of Americans who aren't sure where they lie on a liberal-conservative scale also say they aren't sure where they fall on a left-right scale. The other 29% fall across the political spectrum: 6% say they are left-of-center, 9% say they are right-of-center, and 14% say their politics are centrist.

Looked at in reverse, 79% of Americans who call themselves "far left" describe themselves as "very liberal," compared to 26% of the "left" and 1% of the "center-left." 77% of the "far right" say they're "very conservative," as do 26% of the "right" and 6% of the "center-right."

70% of centrists say their politics are "moderate," as do 45% of the "center-left" and 36% of the "center-right."

Less than 10% of the far left, left, right, and far right each call themselves moderate.

Most Americans (76%) say the word "liberal" always or sometimes means someone whose politics are on the left side of the political spectrum; only 6% say it never does. But there are big differences between those who say liberal *always* means left (41% of all U.S. adult citizens) and those who say it *sometimes* does (48%).

Right-of-center Americans are especially likely to say that "liberal" is a synonym for left: 63% say that, compared to 28% who say it only sometimes is. Left-of-center Americans are more split: 45% say "liberal" always means left and 48% say it doesn't. Centrists are much more likely to be not sure (25%) or to say "liberal" sometimes means left (40%) than to say it always does (27%).

Methodology: *This article includes results from online surveys conducted November 18 - 20, 2024, December 19 - 21, 2024, and December 20 - 23, 2024, among 3,288 U.S. adult citizens. Respondents were selected from YouGov's opt-in panel to be representative of adult U.S. citizens. The sample was weighted according to gender, age, race, education, 2024 presidential vote, 2020 election turnout and presidential vote, baseline party identification, and current voter registration status. 2024 presidential vote, at time of weighting, was estimated to be 48% Harris and 50% Trump. Demographic weighting targets come from the 2019 American Community Survey. Baseline party identification is the respondent's most* *recent answer given around November 8, 2024, and is weighted to the estimated distribution at that time (31% Democratic, 32% Republican). The margin of error for the overall sample is approximately 2.5%.*

How The (Mythical) Left-Right Political Spectrum Harms America

Although most people would agree that American politics has become more toxic in recent years, there is much less agreement on why that is. One common answer is that our parties are moving to the extremes, with the Democrats moving leftward on the political spectrum and the Republicans moving more right. In *The Myth of Left and Right: How the Political Spectrum Misleads and Harms America* we argue that this is incorrect and that, in fact, it's the very conceptualization of politics in terms of a political spectrum that is itself causing much of our political dysfunction.

As the political spectrum has risen in popularity and prominence, the vitriol of public discourse has risen right along with it. Ideas have consequences, and a misleading political paradigm has led to inaccurate political thinking. It's not that America or our parties have moved leftward or rightward on an imaginary line; it's that left-right thinking itself leads us into all kinds of errors that inflame and exacerbate the misunderstandings and tribal hatreds that are characteristic of democratic politics.

For most of our history, Americans didn't think in terms of a spectrum. They just saw (accurately) that America had a two-party system and that each of these parties stood for a bundle of unrelated positions. This all started to change after World War I when Americans imported the left-right model that had arisen in Europe during the French Revolution. Since then, the use of the spectrum has grown exponentially and actual policy has been obscured as Americans have become accustomed to placing every person, institution, or group somewhere on a left-right scale (with radicals on the far left, progressives and liberals on the center left, reactionaries on the far right, and conservatives on the center right). The political spectrum is, without question, the most common political paradigm in 21st-century America.

The central problem with this model is that it's inaccurate for the simple reason that there's more than one issue in politics and a spectrum can, by definition, measure only one issue. There are a multitude of distinct, unrelated political policies under consideration today (e.g., abortion, income taxes, affirmative action, drug control, gun control, health care spending, the minimum wage, military intervention, etc.), and yet our predominant political model presumes that there is just one.

So if there is more than one issue in politics, why do Americans use a unidimensional political spectrum to describe politics? Generally, it's because they are convinced that there is one essential issue that underlies and binds all others, such as "change," and therefore the political spectrum accurately models where someone stands in relation to this essence. Their position on the change (left) vs. preservation (right) issue determines what views they will have on all other issues. If someone is mildly opposed to change (conservative or center right), then they will mildly oppose all the individual policies that promote change (abortion rights, tax increases, etc.), and this will, in turn, lead them to associate with the conservative tribe that shares their views.

We contend that this is exactly backward. There is no essential issue underlying all others—abortion and tax rates really are distinct and unrelated policies—and socialization, not essence, explains the correlation between them. People first anchor into a tribe (because of peers, family, or a single issue they feel strongly about), adopt the positions of the tribe as a matter of socialization, and only then reverse engineer a story about how all the positions of their tribe are united by some essential principle (e.g., progressivism or conservatism). For instance, someone who feels strongly about the right to life (perhaps because of upbringing, religion, or a psychological disposition) will then anchor into the tribe that opposes abortion, adopt its other issues (such as tax cuts) as a matter of socialization, and then explain, after the fact, that both opposing abortion and favoring tax cuts somehow "conserves." Left-right ideology is the fiction we use to justify and mask our tribal attachments.

But many of those who concede that left-right ideologies are social rather than essential nonetheless maintain that we should keep using the political spectrum because it is "useful." An imperfect model, they say, is better than no model at all, and the political spectrum is a simple heuristic that allows us to better navigate the political landscape.

The problem with this view is that it lacks evidence. Would it be useful for medical doctors to model all illnesses, treatments, and patients on a spectrum? Obviously not because medicine is multidimensional and trying to model all medical issues using a single dimension would do great harm. The same is true of politics. Doctors get along just fine by talking about specific illnesses and treatments (lung cancer, fractured tibia, bronchial infection, chemotherapy, bone setting, antibiotics), and political discourse would be much more productive if we simply talked about specific political problems and policies (crime, poverty, inflation, gun control, welfare spending, interest-rate tightening).

Yes, all models are simplifications of reality, but those models must also be accurate such that they improve rather than hinder our understanding of the matter in question. A bad model is actually worse than no model at all (as the four humors theory of disease makes clear), and the political spectrum is a bad model. It is a tool of misinformation, false association, and hostility.

For instance, it's conventional wisdom today that the Republican Party has moved to the right in recent decades. It's also conventional wisdom that small government is right wing, and yet, by every objective measure, Republicans have radically expanded the size of government every time they have been in power over the past two decades. The political spectrum is deceiving us about the behavior of our public officials. Republicans today are far more in favor of racial equality, gay marriage, and government intervention in the economy than they were 50 years ago, and yet the political spectrum tells us they have moved "to the right." How is the political spectrum useful for understanding the evolution of the Republican Party? It is not.

Instead of making simplistic claims about the parties moving leftward or rightward on an imaginary line, we in higher education should think as we do in every other realm of life and be specific. We talk about recreation in granular terms (there is mountain biking, playing chess, watching movies, playing video games, road biking, oil painting, etc.), so why is it too much to ask for us to be similarly granular when talking politics? Instead of saying, "She's on the far left," we should say, "She's an environmentalist." Instead of saying, "He's on the center right," we should say, "He's an anti-Trump Republican." Going granular provides accurate information whereas talking about where people, ideas, and institutions fit on a spectrum simply confuses and inflames. And if we want to refer to what group someone belongs to, "Democrat" and "Republican" work just fine (as do "blue" and "red") and don't carry any of the false essentialist connotations of "conservative" and "liberal." Talking in terms of a spectrum serves no informational function, but it does serve to elevate the temperature of debate and make the public really angry about the "commies" or "fascists" on the other side.

Since part of the mission of Heterodox Academy is to open up productive debate between people who disagree, then the organization should lead the way in jettisoning this political model that makes constructive disagreement difficult. When we presume that left and right are worldviews, we are much less willing to engage and listen to those in the other tribe (after all, their positions all grow out of an evil overarching worldview and therefore they must all be incorrect). If someone is under the delusion, for instance, that all the policies considered left wing are bound by the essence of social justice or progress, then they can't compromise or revise their views without also promoting social injustice and regress. If, on the other hand, they saw left wing and right wing for what they are—tribes who stand for baskets of unrelated positions—then they would be open to find, through rational investigation and open dialogue, which political issues are correct, incorrect, or (even more likely) misconceived entirely. Perhaps the single best way to improve the quality of public discourse is to shed the destructive fiction that all the positions of one's own side are bound by a correct philosophy and therefore all correct a priori.

Of course America has a two-party system, but we should give up the fiction that all the policies of each party are bound by some underlying essence (left-progressivism or right-conservatism). Parties are incoherent baskets of issues—some good, some bad—and we do ourselves no favors by concocting ex post stories that give the illusion of coherence to these random policies thrown together by historical accident. It's time we confronted the simple reality that, yes, there are many distinct, unrelated issues in politics and so, no, we can't profitably model these many distinct issues on a unidimensional spectrum.

A **centrist** is someone whose political beliefs and positions fall somewhere in the middle of the political spectrum, blending ideas from both the **left** and the **right**. Centrists typically seek a balanced approach to political and social issues, often prioritizing **pragmatism** and **compromise** over rigid ideological purity. They tend to value **moderation, consensus-building**, and **incremental change** rather than radical or extreme shifts in policy.

Here's a breakdown of what it means to be a centrist:

---

1. Economic Policies

- **Balanced Approach**: Centrists often support a mix of **market-driven economics** (favoring free markets and private enterprise) with elements of **government regulation** and **social welfare** to address inequality and provide a safety net.

- **Support for Mixed Economy**: They may advocate for **capitalism** but believe in **government intervention** when necessary to prevent excessive inequality, regulate industries, and promote public services like healthcare and education.

- **Fiscal Responsibility**: Centrists often stress the importance of balancing **economic growth** with **budgetary discipline** and may support policies that aim to reduce government debt while also funding necessary social programs.

2. Social Issues

- **Moderate Social Policies**: Centrists tend to support **individual rights** but also value **social stability**. They might back progressive changes on issues like **gender equality**, **LGBTQ+ rights**, and **racial equality**, but prefer gradual reforms rather than sweeping changes.

- **Social Tolerance**: They support tolerance and inclusivity but may be more cautious about some radical social changes, seeking common ground on issues like **marriage equality** or **immigration**.

- **Balancing Tradition and Progress**: Centrists may look for ways to respect cultural traditions while also promoting equality and justice.

---

3. Role of Government

- **Limited but Active Government**: Centrists usually favor a government that plays a **moderate role** in regulating the economy, providing public services, and ensuring social justice, while also respecting **individual freedoms**.

- **Government Efficiency**: They often advocate for policies that make government **more efficient and transparent**, avoiding excessive bureaucracy or government overreach.

4. Foreign Policy

- **Pragmatic Diplomacy**: Centrists typically support **international cooperation** and **diplomacy**, aiming for **global stability** while also prioritizing **national interests**. They may advocate for multilateral institutions (e.g., UN, NATO) but are also pragmatic about the need for national sovereignty and security.

- **Balanced Defense & Diplomacy**: They may support maintaining a strong national defense while engaging in diplomatic efforts to resolve conflicts and promote peace.

5. Environmental Policy

- **Sensible Environmentalism**: Centrists often favor **environmental protection** but with policies that are **economically feasible**. They may support **green energy** and **sustainable practices** while balancing these goals with **economic growth** and **job creation** in sectors like fossil fuels and manufacturing.

- **Climate Change**: While acknowledging climate change as a serious issue, centrists may advocate for **pragmatic solutions** that do not overly burden businesses or the economy.

6. Immigration and National Identity

- **Balanced Immigration Policies**: Centrists tend to support **immigration reform** that strikes a balance between **humanitarian concerns** and **national security**. They may advocate for pathways to citizenship for immigrants while ensuring that immigration laws are fair and manageable.

- **National Unity**: They often believe in preserving national identity while welcoming diversity, valuing both **cultural heritage** and **multiculturalism**.

---

7. Political Style and Strategy

- **Pragmatism Over Ideology**: Centrists often emphasize **compromise** and **bipartisanship**. They are more likely to be open to **working across party lines** to find common solutions rather than adhering strictly to a particular political ideology.

- **Focus on Problem-Solving**: Centrists often view political debates as opportunities for finding **practical, middle-ground solutions** to problems rather than ideological battles.

- **Appeal to a Broad Voter Base**: Because of their moderate stance, centrists may appeal to voters from across the political spectrum, seeking to unite **diverse groups** rather than appeal to one side of the political divide.

Summary of Centrist Views

- **Economic Views**: Mix of market-driven policies and government regulation to ensure fairness and economic stability.

- **Social Issues**: Moderation on social change, balancing progress with tradition.

- **Government Role**: Government should provide services and protections but be efficient and avoid overreach.

- **Foreign Policy**: Emphasis on diplomacy and international cooperation, while prioritizing national security.

- **Environment**: Support for sustainable environmental policies that balance economic considerations.

- **Political Approach**: Seek compromise and pragmatic solutions, often working across party lines.

Centrist Political Movements

Centrism is often represented by **moderate parties** or individuals within larger political systems. Some examples include:

- **The Third Way**: A political approach championed by leaders like **Bill Clinton** and **Tony Blair** that aimed to combine free-market policies with social democratic values.

- **Moderate Democrats/Republicans (U.S.)**: In the U.S., centrists may refer to moderate members of the **Democratic Party** or **Republican Party**, those who do not adhere to the extreme ends of their respective parties.

- **The Liberal Democrats (UK)**: A centrist party in the UK that blends socially liberal policies with market-friendly economics.

Conclusion

A **centrist** is someone who tends to hold a middle-ground position between the extremes of the left and right, valuing moderation, compromise, and practical solutions. They focus on **balancing individual freedoms with social justice**, and **economic efficiency with sustainability**, often seeking to **bridge divides** between conflicting political ideologies.

Centrist policies aim to blend elements from both **left-wing** and **right-wing** ideologies, creating practical solutions that balance different values and priorities. The goal is often to find common ground between competing ideas and to address issues in a way that is **economically viable**, **socially equitable**, and **politically inclusive**. Centrist policies typically avoid extreme positions and prioritize **compromise**, **pragmatism**, and **incremental reform**.

Here's a breakdown of some common **centrist policies** in various areas:

---

1. Economic Policies

- **Mixed Economy**: Centrists support a **mixed economy** that combines the **efficiency** of **market-driven capitalism** with **government intervention** to ensure social welfare and regulate industries. This includes policies like:
    - **Support for free markets**, but with regulations to prevent monopolies and protect consumers.
    - **Progressive taxation** to fund essential social services (e.g., healthcare, education) without excessively taxing the middle class or stifling economic growth.
    - **Support for small businesses** and entrepreneurs, while ensuring that larger

corporations adhere to ethical labor practices and environmental standards.

- **Balanced budget**: Centrists advocate for **fiscal responsibility**, aiming to reduce budget deficits and public debt over time while also ensuring sufficient investment in public goods.

2. Social Policies

- **Health and Education**:
  - **Affordable healthcare** for all, often through a **hybrid system** where the government provides basic coverage while private insurance remains an option.
  - **Accessible education** with a focus on quality public schools, affordable college, and technical training programs to ensure equal opportunities for all citizens.
  - **Public-private partnerships** to expand access to essential services while promoting innovation in sectors like healthcare and education.

- **Social Safety Net**:
  - Support for programs like **unemployment benefits, disability assistance**, and **social security** that provide a safety net for those in

need, but with **measures to prevent dependency** and encourage self-sufficiency.

- **Conditional welfare programs** that require recipients to seek work or participate in job training programs to receive support.

3. Environmental Policies

- **Pragmatic Environmentalism**: Centrists support **environmental protections** but seek solutions that also allow for **economic growth** and **job creation**. This includes:
    - **Investment in renewable energy** (e.g., solar, wind) while balancing the transition with support for industries affected by the shift away from fossil fuels.
    - **Carbon emissions reduction** strategies that combine **market incentives** (e.g., carbon pricing) with **regulatory measures** to curb pollution.
    - Support for **sustainable agriculture** and **conservation** practices to protect natural resources while ensuring that food production remains efficient and affordable.

4. Foreign and Defense Policies

- **Diplomacy First**: Centrists tend to prioritize **diplomatic engagement** and **international cooperation** while also maintaining a strong national defense. Key aspects include:

    - **Multilateralism**: Supporting institutions like the **United Nations**, **World Trade Organization**, and **NATO** to address global challenges such as security, climate change, and human rights.

    - **Balanced Defense Spending**: Maintaining a **strong military** for national security but seeking ways to **limit defense spending** without compromising safety.

    - **Trade and Globalization**: Advocating for **free trade agreements** that benefit all parties while addressing the need to protect domestic industries and jobs. They also favor **global solutions** to issues like **climate change**, **pandemics**, and **human rights**.

---

5. Social Issues

- **Gender Equality and LGBTQ+ Rights**: Centrists support **equality** for all genders and sexual orientations while seeking to respect cultural or religious differences. They might support policies such as:

- o **Marriage equality** for LGBTQ+ individuals.
- o Laws to **protect against discrimination** based on gender, sexuality, and other identity factors.
- o **Workplace equality** measures to ensure that men and women receive equal pay for equal work and have access to the same opportunities.

- **Immigration**:
    - o **Balanced immigration policies** that provide a path to citizenship for those who contribute to society while ensuring that immigration laws are fair, efficient, and respect the sovereignty of the nation.
    - o **Pathways to citizenship** for undocumented immigrants who have been in the country for a long period, while also securing borders and addressing national security concerns.

6. Criminal Justice Reform

- **Criminal Justice System**: Centrists typically support **reforms** to ensure fairness and reduce inequalities within the criminal justice system:
    - o Support for **police reform** to ensure that law enforcement treats all citizens equally while also providing the police with the necessary tools and training to maintain public safety.

- Advocacy for **rehabilitation over incarceration** for non-violent offenders, especially for issues like drug addiction.
- Measures to address **mass incarceration** and **racial disparities** in arrests and sentencing while ensuring that laws are enforced effectively.

7. Political Reforms

- **Electoral Reform**:
    - Support for **electoral reforms** that increase voter participation and transparency, such as **ranked-choice voting** or **campaign finance reforms** to reduce the influence of big money in politics.
    - **Bipartisanship**: Centrists generally advocate for **compromise** and cooperation between political parties to address national challenges. They may push for **cross-party collaboration** on issues like healthcare, immigration, and infrastructure.
- **Decentralization**:
    - Support for a **balance of power** between federal, state, and local governments to ensure that decisions are made at the level closest to the people while maintaining strong federal oversight on national issues.

8. Technology and Innovation

- **Support for Innovation**: Centrists often support policies that foster **technological innovation** while also protecting individuals' rights and security. This includes:

    - **Data protection** and **privacy laws** to ensure that people's personal information is protected in the digital age.

    - Encouraging **public-private partnerships** to fund research and development in areas like healthcare, renewable energy, and technology.

    - **Tech regulation**: Support for regulating major tech companies to prevent monopolies and ensure that they act in the public interest without stifling innovation.

Summary of Centrist Policies

Centrists typically advocate for **pragmatic, balanced policies** that:

- Combine market efficiency with social protections.

- Seek **moderate reforms** on social issues without drastic shifts.
- Support **international cooperation** while maintaining national security.
- Address **environmental challenges** while promoting economic growth.
- Ensure **criminal justice reforms** and uphold **individual rights**.

The centrist approach often favors **incremental changes** over radical shifts, focusing on **practical solutions** that can be broadly supported across the political spectrum.

Centrist policies in action are often seen in countries and regions where governments seek to balance economic growth with social welfare, while fostering both **individual freedoms** and **social equity**. Below are some examples of centrist policies in practice, highlighting how they manifest in various areas of governance.

---

1. Economic Policies

Example: The Third Way (Clinton & Blair)

- **Background**: The **Third Way** was a centrist political approach adopted by leaders like **Bill Clinton** (U.S.) and **Tony Blair** (UK) in the 1990s. It was designed to combine the social policies of the left with the market-driven policies of the right.

- **Policies in Action**:
    - **Welfare-to-Work Programs**: Clinton's administration introduced **welfare reform** aimed at encouraging people to seek employment rather than rely on long-term government assistance. This reform balanced **personal responsibility** with necessary social safety nets.
    - **Economic Growth with Regulation**: Both Clinton and Blair promoted economic growth by supporting free-market policies like **trade liberalization** and **technology innovation**, while also increasing investment in education and healthcare.

2. Healthcare

Example: Affordable Care Act (Obamacare, U.S.)

- **Background**: The **Affordable Care Act (ACA)**, signed into law by President **Barack Obama** in 2010, is a **centrist healthcare reform** that aimed to increase **health insurance coverage** while moderating costs.

- **Policies in Action**:
    - The ACA created **market-based solutions** for expanding access to healthcare, such as **healthcare exchanges** for people to shop for insurance plans and **subsidies** to make health insurance more affordable.
    - It also introduced **Medicaid expansion** in some states, aiming to reduce the uninsured population, but it did so in a way that relied on both **private insurers** and **government intervention**.
    - Rather than implementing a fully socialized healthcare system, the ACA embraced a hybrid approach that incorporated both **private and public sector involvement**.

3. Social Policies

Example: Marriage Equality (Various Countries)

- **Background**: **Marriage equality** is a major social issue where centrists have played a role in advancing **LGBTQ+ rights** while balancing public opinion and traditional values.

- **Policies in Action**:
    - In many countries (e.g., **the United States, Ireland, Australia**), marriage equality has been achieved through a combination of **legal changes** and **public referenda** or **parliamentary votes** that respected both **individual rights** and societal norms.
    - **Incremental Progress**: Many centrists prefer to pass marriage equality laws after **public dialogue** and ensuring that protections for religious institutions and businesses are included. This compromise approach avoids a more confrontational, rapid change while ensuring equal rights for LGBTQ+ people.

---

4. Environmental Policies

Example: Paris Climate Agreement (2015)

- **Background**: The **Paris Climate Agreement** is a global treaty where governments, including many centrist leaders, agreed to take steps to **limit global**

warming to well below 2°C compared to pre-industrial levels.

- **Policies in Action**:
    - The agreement allows for **nationally determined contributions** (NDCs), meaning countries set their own **climate goals** and policies but are held accountable to meet them. This is a centrist approach that balances **global cooperation** with **national sovereignty**.
    - It focuses on both **economic development** and **environmental protection**, ensuring that countries can pursue green technologies and energy sources without jeopardizing economic growth.

---

5. Immigration Policies

Example: Comprehensive Immigration Reform (U.S.)

- **Background**: U.S. centrists often support **immigration reforms** that provide a path to citizenship for undocumented immigrants, while also strengthening border security and enforcing immigration laws.

- **Policies in Action**:
    - **Dream Act (2012)**: This was a significant centrist policy supported by both Democrats and Republicans to provide a pathway to legal

status for **undocumented immigrants** who came to the U.S. as children, also known as "Dreamers."

- **Border Security + Path to Citizenship**: Centrists often advocate for a balanced approach that includes **strong border security** alongside **comprehensive immigration reform** that allows for legal pathways for immigrants, like temporary work visas and citizenship for long-term residents.

---

6. Criminal Justice Reform

Example: Sentencing Reform (Bipartisan Support in U.S.)

- **Background**: Centrist policies have played a significant role in **criminal justice reform**, particularly in addressing **mass incarceration** and **discriminatory practices** in the justice system.
- **Policies in Action**:
  - The **First Step Act** (2018) is a **bipartisan** law in the U.S. aimed at reducing **mandatory minimum sentences** for non-violent offenders, expanding **rehabilitation programs** for prisoners, and providing

prisoners with better opportunities for early release based on good behavior.

- **Restorative Justice**: Centrist policies advocate for combining **punishment** with **rehabilitation**, aiming to reduce recidivism and address the root causes of crime like **poverty** and **mental health issues**.

---

7. Foreign Policy

Example: Multilateral Trade Agreements

- **Background**: Many centrist governments support **free trade agreements** that allow for international cooperation, while protecting local industries and ensuring fair trade practices.

- **Policies in Action**:

    - The **North American Free Trade Agreement (NAFTA)** (1994), and its successor, the **United States-Mexico-Canada Agreement (USMCA)** (2020), were centrist policies that aimed to increase trade between the U.S., Mexico, and Canada while ensuring that labor and environmental standards were met.

    - These agreements are often designed to be **economically beneficial** for all parties, with provisions to protect **intellectual property**, address **trade imbalances**, and establish **dispute resolution mechanisms**.

8. Technology and Innovation

Example: Data Protection Laws (EU's GDPR)

- **Background**: Centrist policies often try to balance the needs of consumers with the needs of businesses in the rapidly evolving **digital economy**.

- **Policies in Action**:
    - The **General Data Protection Regulation (GDPR)**, implemented by the European Union in 2018, regulates how businesses collect, store, and use personal data. It ensures **data privacy rights** for individuals while allowing companies to continue operating in the digital space.
    - By combining strong **privacy protections** with **clear regulations** on digital marketing and data collection, GDPR is a centrist policy that addresses the modern concerns of digital ethics and business needs.

9. Education Policies

Example: Universal Pre-K (Various States, U.S.)

- **Background**: Many centrist politicians support the idea of **universal pre-kindergarten education** as a way to ensure early childhood education is available to all families, regardless of income.

- **Policies in Action**:
  - **State-led initiatives**, such as in **New York** and **California**, have introduced **public pre-K programs** that ensure all children have access to quality early education, without making it a fully government-run system, thereby respecting **parental choice** and **private education**.
  - **Public-private partnerships** often help fund these initiatives, ensuring that there is sufficient infrastructure while also encouraging local businesses to support educational programs.

Summary of Centrist Policies in Action

- **Pragmatism and compromise** are key to centrist policies, as they try to balance the competing priorities of both **economic growth** and **social justice**.

- **Incremental reform** rather than radical change is often favored, especially when it comes to social policies (e.g., marriage equality, healthcare reform).

- **Multilateral cooperation** and **market-driven solutions** are common in international and environmental policies (e.g., climate agreements, trade deals).

- **Bipartisan support** is central to the success of centrist policies, as they seek to bring together different political viewpoints for effective governance (e.g., criminal justice reform, immigration reform).

The term **"woke"** in America has evolved over time and has been widely used in political, cultural, and social discourse. Originally, **"woke"** referred to an awareness of social injustices, especially related to **racial inequality**, **discrimination**, and **human rights**. However, in recent years, the meaning has broadened and become a subject of intense debate and sometimes controversy.

Here's a breakdown of how the term **"woke"** is used, both positively and negatively, in contemporary America:

---

1. Historical Context of "Woke"

- **Origins**: The term **"woke"** has its roots in African American vernacular English (AAVE) and originally meant being aware of and sensitive to social and racial issues, particularly **systemic racism** and **racial injustice**.

- **Early Usage**: In the mid-20th century, **"woke"** was often used in activist circles to describe a heightened sense of awareness regarding racial inequality, particularly within the context of the **Civil Rights Movement** and the **Black Power** movement. For example, the phrase "stay woke" was popularized by civil rights activists and was a call to remain vigilant about social injustices.

---

2. Contemporary Usage and Cultural Shift

Over time, the concept of **being woke** has expanded to cover a broader set of social and political issues beyond just race.

- **Social Justice Movements**: Today, **woke** is often associated with an increased awareness of various **social justice** issues, including:
    - **Gender equality** (e.g., feminism, the rights of transgender individuals)
    - **LGBTQ+ rights** (e.g., marriage equality, combating discrimination)
    - **Economic inequality** (e.g., addressing poverty and wealth disparity)
    - **Environmental justice** (e.g., addressing climate change and its impacts on marginalized communities)
- **"Woke Culture"**: The term has come to describe a broader **cultural phenomenon** where individuals and institutions advocate for **progressive social policies, political correctness**, and **identity politics**. It involves the active promotion of inclusivity and equality in various aspects of life, such as workplaces, education, media, and entertainment.

3. Criticism and Controversy

As the term **woke** has become more mainstream, it has also become a target of criticism, especially from those who feel that it represents an overreach or imposition of certain progressive ideologies.

- **Woke as a Pejorative**: In the past few years, particularly on the **right-wing** of American politics, the term **woke** has been used pejoratively. Critics argue that **"wokeness"** represents an extreme form of political correctness, **cancel culture**, or **virtue signaling**, where individuals or organizations may embrace progressive views not out of genuine concern, but to gain social approval or avoid criticism.

    - **"Cancel Culture"**: Critics of wokeness often associate it with **cancel culture**, which involves publicly shaming or boycotting individuals or companies for perceived offensive behavior, past actions, or statements. This is viewed by some as excessive and harmful to free speech.

    - **Overzealousness**: Some argue that **woke culture** goes too far, focusing too heavily on minute issues or punishing people for unintentional mistakes, and that it stifles honest conversation and debate. They claim that the emphasis on being "woke" can sometimes overshadow the real, substantive issues facing marginalized communities.

- **Economic & Cultural Shifts**: Another criticism from the right is that woke policies, particularly in the areas of **education** and **corporate governance**, have led to a focus on **identity politics** at the expense of broader economic and social concerns. Some feel that initiatives like **diversity quotas** or **affirmative action** may undermine merit-based systems.

4. Woke Politics and Identity Politics

The rise of "woke" culture is often tied to **identity politics**, which refers to political movements and social advocacy that are based on the shared experiences of specific groups, such as those based on **race**, **gender**, **sexual orientation**, or **disability**.

- **Identity Politics**: Supporters of "woke" policies argue that identity politics are necessary to address systemic inequalities. They believe that focusing on the experiences of marginalized groups is essential to achieving true equality, as these groups often face disproportionate levels of discrimination and disadvantage.

- **Affirmative Action**: Support for policies like **affirmative action** is often associated with the woke movement. Proponents argue that such policies help redress historical injustices, especially in areas like education and employment, by ensuring that marginalized groups have equal access to opportunities.

5. "Woke" in the Media and Entertainment

- **Representation and Inclusivity**: Hollywood, the media, and entertainment industries have increasingly embraced the idea of **inclusivity** and **representation** in response to "woke" culture. This has led to a broader focus on **diverse voices** and **stories** in film, television, and literature, as well as calls for more equitable representation in casting, directing, and producing roles.

- **Content Warnings and Sensitivity**: Many institutions have implemented **content warnings** or **sensitivity reviews** for their productions to ensure that they do not perpetuate harmful stereotypes or overlook marginalized groups. While some view these efforts as important steps toward inclusivity, others argue that they limit creative freedom.

6. Woke in Politics

- **Progressive Politics**: The term "woke" is often associated with **progressive political movements** in the U.S., including **left-wing** activists, **Democratic Party** members, and figures like **Bernie Sanders, Alexandria Ocasio-Cortez**, and other members of **The Squad** who advocate for policies that address **climate change, healthcare** reform, **universal education**, and **racial and social justice**.

- **The "Woke Left"**: Opponents of progressive movements often use the term "woke" to refer to the more radical elements of the **left-wing**, accusing them of promoting social policies that are overly idealistic or divisive.
    - **Examples**: Calls for **defunding the police**, **universal basic income**, **green new deal** policies, and **open borders** immigration reforms are often framed as examples of "woke" political ideology.
- **Moderates and Centrists**: Some moderate Democrats and centrists in the U.S. push back against the **woke left**, arguing that **pragmatism** and **compromise** are necessary for political success. They may believe that **extreme** or **divisive** views associated with woke politics could alienate voters in swing states or lead to political polarization.

---

7. "Woke" in Corporate America

- **Corporate Wokeness**: In response to consumer demand for **social responsibility**, many companies have embraced "woke" principles, implementing diversity and inclusion initiatives, promoting sustainable practices, and taking stances on various social issues like **racial equality**, **LGBTQ+ rights**, and **climate change**.

- **Brand Activism**: Companies like **Nike**, **Ben & Jerry's**, and **Amazon** have publicly supported movements like **Black Lives Matter** and pushed for progressive reforms. Some see this as genuine support for social justice, while others criticize it as **corporate virtue signaling**, accusing companies of using social issues as a marketing tool without enacting real change.

Summary: Woke in America Today

- **Woke as a Positive Force**: For many, being "woke" represents **social awareness**, a commitment to **justice**, and a focus on **equality**, particularly regarding **race**, **gender**, **sexuality**, and **economic inequality**. It's seen as a call to address deep-seated societal issues, and it encourages people to stay vigilant and proactive in promoting fairness.

- **Woke as Controversial**: On the other hand, many critics argue that being "woke" can sometimes go too far in its focus on **political correctness** or **identity politics**, and can even alienate or divide people rather than promote unity. The idea of "cancel culture," **over-sensitivity**, and the use of "woke" as a pejorative are part of this backlash.

In the end, whether one views **woke** culture positively or negatively often depends on their political leanings, values, and perspectives on how social change should be achieved.

"Woke" positions in politics today generally refer to the progressive or left-leaning stances on issues related to **social justice**, **identity politics**, and **inclusivity**. These positions are often associated with movements for racial equality, gender justice, LGBTQ+ rights, economic reform, and climate action. Politicians and activists who are described as "woke" tend to advocate for policies that challenge traditional power structures and aim to address systemic inequalities. Below are some of the key "woke" positions in modern politics:

---

1. Racial Justice and Equality

- **Police Reform and Abolition**: Many politicians, particularly on the left, support reforms aimed at **defunding** or **restructuring** police forces in order to reduce police violence, particularly against Black and marginalized communities. Some take more radical stances, advocating for **abolishing the police** and reallocating resources to community-based solutions (e.g., mental health services, community policing).
    - **Black Lives Matter**: The movement advocating for racial justice in law enforcement has been one of the central rallying points for woke positions. Calls to address **systemic racism**, end **racial profiling**, and implement policies to reduce racial disparities in the criminal justice system are key to this movement.

- **Affirmative Action**: A woke position supports policies that ensure **underrepresented racial and ethnic groups** have equal access to opportunities in areas like education, employment, and housing. Affirmative action is often framed as a necessary tool to address historical **discrimination** and create a more equitable society.

---

2. Gender and LGBTQ+ Rights

- **Gender Equality and Reproductive Rights**: Woke politics frequently prioritize **gender equality** by advocating for women's rights, including access to **abortion**, **birth control**, and **reproductive healthcare**. Efforts are also made to address the **gender wage gap**, promote **equal representation** in leadership roles, and combat **gender-based violence**.

    - Woke activists also strongly support **transgender rights**, advocating for laws that protect transgender individuals from discrimination in areas like **employment**, **education**, and **healthcare**. They also push for policies that allow for **gender self-identification** and better healthcare services for transgender people.

- **LGBTQ+ Rights**: Woke positions in politics strongly advocate for **LGBTQ+ rights**, including **marriage equality**, **anti-discrimination laws**, and the **right** to **gender-affirming healthcare**. The movement seeks to protect LGBTQ+ individuals from discrimination in employment, housing, and education, as well as challenge harmful policies like **conversion therapy**.

3. Economic Justice and Redistribution

- **Wealth Inequality and Taxes**: Woke political positions often align with efforts to address **economic inequality** by advocating for progressive tax policies, higher taxes on the wealthy, and policies aimed at redistributing wealth. These include proposals like **universal basic income (UBI)**, **wealth taxes**, and expanding **social safety nets** (e.g., expanded healthcare, affordable housing, universal childcare).

- **Labor Rights**: Woke positions tend to emphasize workers' rights, including support for **unionization**, raising the **minimum wage**, improving working conditions, and ensuring **living wages**. There is also support for **workers' rights to organize** in sectors like **tech**, **gig work**, and **service industries**.

4. Climate Justice and Environmentalism

- **Climate Change Action**: Woke politics strongly advocate for policies to combat **climate change**. This includes supporting policies like the **Green**

New Deal, which calls for large-scale investments in renewable energy, green jobs, and infrastructure improvements to mitigate the impacts of climate change.

   - The concept of **climate justice** is also a core element, emphasizing that the poorest and most marginalized communities are often the most affected by environmental degradation. Woke activists argue for policies that address the unequal impact of climate change on **low-income** and **communities of color**.

- **Environmental Justice**: Woke positions on environmental issues advocate for efforts to reduce environmental hazards in marginalized communities, ensuring that communities of color and economically disadvantaged areas are not disproportionately burdened by **pollution, toxic waste**, or **climate disasters**.

5. Immigration and Refugee Rights

- **Open Borders and Immigration Reform**: A key woke political position involves advocating for more inclusive and humane immigration policies, including **pathways to citizenship** for undocumented immigrants, the protection of **DACA recipients**, and abolishing policies like **family separation** at the U.S.-Mexico border.

- There is also strong support for **refugee** and **asylum seeker** rights, advocating for policies that provide safe havens for people fleeing conflict or persecution and ensuring that **human rights** are respected in immigration enforcement.

6. Anti-Colonialism and Indigenous Rights

- **Indigenous Sovereignty**: Woke politics often focus on advocating for the **rights** and **sovereignty** of Indigenous peoples. This includes supporting **land rights**, **cultural preservation**, and **self-determination** for Indigenous communities.
  - **De-colonization** efforts are also central to woke positions, which challenge ongoing systems of colonialism that persist in many modern societies. This includes reexamining historical events (e.g., the **removal of statues of historical figures** associated with colonialism and slavery) and supporting reparations for Indigenous communities.

7. Cancel Culture and Free Speech

- **Cancel Culture**: Woke politics is often associated with the rise of **cancel culture**, where individuals or institutions are publicly shamed or boycotted for engaging in **offensive** or **harmful** behavior. This may include speaking out against people who hold prejudiced or discriminatory views, or who have made statements in the past that are now considered problematic.

  - Supporters argue that **accountability** is necessary to challenge oppressive ideologies, while critics contend that it stifles free speech and can lead to **overreaction** or **punishment** for minor infractions.

- **Political Correctness**: Woke positions often champion the use of **inclusive language** and **political correctness**, emphasizing respect for all identities and experiences. While this approach seeks to foster a culture of respect and empathy, critics argue that it can lead to **censorship** and a **lack of open debate**.

---

8. Defunding and Reforming Institutions

- **Defunding the Police**: Woke political positions are often aligned with calls to **defund** or **reform** police forces. This position advocates for reallocating funds from police departments to community services such as **mental health crisis response**, **education**, and **housing**.

  - Supporters believe that police forces often over-police marginalized communities and perpetuate violence, particularly against **Black** and **brown** people. They argue that by investing in community-based alternatives, public safety can be improved without relying on traditional law enforcement.

- **Abolitionism**: Some activists take a more radical position by advocating for the **abolition** of not just the police, but also other institutions of social control, such as **prisons** and **the criminal justice system** itself. Instead, they advocate for restorative justice and alternatives to punitive measures.

9. Education and Critical Race Theory (CRT)

- **Critical Race Theory (CRT)**: Woke positions in education often support the inclusion of **Critical Race Theory** (CRT) in curricula, particularly at the higher education level. CRT examines how **racism** and **white supremacy** are embedded in social, political, and legal systems. Supporters argue that understanding and addressing structural racism is necessary to achieving true equality.
    - However, CRT has become highly controversial, especially in K-12 education, where opponents argue that it encourages **divisiveness** and promotes a **victim mentality**.

10. Universal Healthcare

- **Medicare for All**: Many who identify with woke politics advocate for **universal healthcare**, often in the form of a **Medicare for All** system. This proposal seeks to provide **free** or **low-cost** healthcare to all individuals, ensuring that no one is excluded from medical care due to their **income** or **insurance status**.

- The idea is rooted in the belief that **healthcare is a human right**, and that access to medical services should not be based on one's ability to pay.

Summary of Woke Positions in Politics Today

Woke positions in contemporary American politics are driven by the pursuit of **justice**, **equality**, and **inclusivity**. They challenge traditional power structures and focus on the lived experiences of marginalized communities, seeking to create a more **equitable** and **inclusive society**. Supporters view these positions as necessary steps toward rectifying historical and systemic inequalities, while critics often argue that they can go too far, causing **division** and **censorship**.

DEI stands for **Diversity, Equity, and Inclusion**. It's a framework that organizations, schools, and governments use to create environments that value and promote diverse perspectives, ensure fair treatment for all individuals, and foster inclusive spaces. Here's a breakdown of each component:

1. Diversity

- Refers to the presence of a wide range of different characteristics in a group. These can include race, ethnicity, gender, age, sexual orientation, disability, religion, socioeconomic background, and more.
- Diversity recognizes and values the differences among people and the perspectives they bring.

2. Equity

- Focuses on ensuring that all individuals have access to the same opportunities, resources, and treatment, but recognizes that people have different needs and may require different support to achieve fairness.
- Unlike equality, which treats everyone the same, equity acknowledges systemic barriers and aims to level the playing field for everyone.

3. Inclusion

- Ensures that all individuals feel respected, valued, and integrated into a group or community. An inclusive environment actively works to make sure everyone, regardless of their background, has a voice and can contribute.

- Inclusion is about creating a culture where diversity is not only present but celebrated, and all people feel empowered to be themselves without fear of discrimination.

DEI in Practice

Organizations and institutions use DEI initiatives to:

- Promote diverse hiring practices.
- Develop policies and programs that eliminate biases or barriers.
- Create inclusive workspaces or communities where everyone feels valued.
- Address systemic inequalities within institutions or society.

DEI is often a part of broader conversations about social justice and addressing inequalities, whether in the workplace, education, or public life.

The focus on **Diversity, Equity, and Inclusion (DEI)** has had significant effects across various sectors in society. While the outcomes can vary depending on the context, there are several broad impacts that DEI efforts have had on individuals, organizations, and society as a whole:

1. Increased Representation and Visibility

- DEI initiatives have led to more diverse representation in areas that were historically dominated by specific groups. This includes greater visibility of women, people of color, LGBTQ+ individuals, and people with disabilities in fields like politics, business leadership, entertainment, and academia.

- This visibility has helped to challenge stereotypes and create more role models for marginalized communities.

2. Improved Workplace Culture

- Organizations that focus on DEI often experience more inclusive work environments, where people from different backgrounds feel valued and supported.

- DEI efforts have helped reduce discrimination, bias, and harassment in workplaces, contributing to a safer, more respectful environment for employees.

- Employees may feel more motivated and engaged in a diverse, inclusive setting, leading to increased collaboration and creativity.

3. Better Decision-Making and Innovation

- Diverse teams tend to be more innovative because they bring a variety of perspectives and experiences. This can result in better problem-solving and decision-making.

- DEI efforts encourage organizations to consider diverse viewpoints when making strategic choices, which can lead to more effective and inclusive solutions.

4. Fairer Access to Opportunities

- Through equity-based policies, DEI aims to eliminate barriers that prevent certain groups from accessing the same opportunities as others. This can be seen in more equitable hiring practices, efforts to close pay gaps, and programs aimed at supporting underrepresented groups in educational institutions and the workforce.

- Efforts to support individuals from disadvantaged backgrounds (e.g., through scholarships, mentorship programs, or tailored support services) help bridge gaps in achievement and access to resources.

5. Social Justice and Addressing Inequality

- DEI is a core part of the broader movement for social justice. It has played a key role in addressing systemic inequality and discrimination in areas like education, healthcare, criminal justice, and housing.

- By highlighting and addressing the unique challenges faced by marginalized communities, DEI initiatives help to move toward a more just and equitable society.

6. Resistance and Controversy

- While many people view DEI efforts as crucial to creating fairer, more inclusive environments, there has also been resistance. Some argue that DEI initiatives can lead to reverse discrimination, or that they prioritize identity over merit.

- Critics may also feel that DEI efforts are too focused on political correctness or that they foster division rather than unity.

- Despite this resistance, DEI continues to be an important focus for many organizations and social movements, as the push for equality and inclusion remains central to societal progress.

7. Cultural Shifts and Public Awareness

- DEI efforts have brought broader attention to issues like racial inequality, gender disparities, and the experiences of LGBTQ+ individuals. This has led to shifts in cultural attitudes and public awareness, encouraging more empathy and understanding.

- Movements like **Black Lives Matter**, **#MeToo**, and others have gained momentum as part of the DEI movement, pushing for changes in policy, corporate practices, and societal attitudes.

8. Education and Awareness

- DEI initiatives have increased awareness about the importance of cultural competence and bias awareness. This has led to more educational programs and training aimed at reducing unconscious bias and promoting respectful interactions.

- Schools and universities have also implemented programs that teach students about the value of diversity, equity, and inclusion, preparing future leaders to navigate diverse and globalized environments.

Challenges:

While DEI has made significant progress, challenges remain. Some of the issues that continue to be debated include:

- Ensuring that DEI efforts lead to meaningful and lasting change rather than being performative.

- Balancing the need for diversity with ensuring qualifications and competence in fields like hiring and promotions.

- Overcoming backlash and resistance to DEI policies in certain contexts, especially where individuals feel their rights or opportunities are being undermined.

In Conclusion:

DEI has influenced many aspects of life, leading to both positive transformations and ongoing challenges. It has fostered greater inclusivity, improved fairness, and promoted social change, but it also continues to spark debate over how best to implement these principles and address the complexities of inequality. As DEI initiatives evolve, they will likely continue to shape the future of workplaces, education, and society at large.

DEI (Diversity, Equity, and Inclusion) in our personal lives can affect us in various ways, shaping our experiences, interactions, and understanding of the world. Here's how DEI might play out in our everyday lives:

1. Personal Relationships and Interactions

- **Diversity:** In our social circles, schools, workplaces, or communities, we interact with people from different backgrounds, cultures, and perspectives. DEI encourages us to appreciate and celebrate these differences, fostering richer, more meaningful relationships.

- **Inclusion:** When we make efforts to include people from diverse backgrounds—whether in conversation, decision-making, or social activities—we contribute to a sense of belonging. This inclusion helps reduce isolation and creates more welcoming environments for others.

- **Equity:** In personal relationships, equity means ensuring that everyone feels heard and treated fairly, regardless of their background or status. It involves being mindful of the privileges we may have and ensuring that others have the same opportunities for growth, respect, and success.

2. Work and School Environments

- **Diversity in the Workplace:** DEI initiatives can shape the work culture by promoting diverse hiring practices and encouraging people from different backgrounds to bring their unique perspectives to the table. This creates a more dynamic and innovative work environment.

- **Equitable Access to Opportunities:** In both work and school, DEI policies seek to remove barriers that may exist for people from underrepresented groups, ensuring that everyone has access to opportunities such as promotions, educational resources, or leadership roles.

- **Inclusive Spaces:** A workplace or school that values inclusion will make efforts to ensure that all individuals feel valued, whether through inclusive language, accessible facilities, or support for various cultural practices and religious observances.

3. Community and Social Justice

- **Raising Awareness:** DEI can influence our engagement with social justice issues, encouraging us to recognize and address inequality in our communities. Whether it's advocating for racial justice, gender equality, or disability rights, DEI pushes us to be more mindful of how societal systems may disadvantage certain groups.

- **Volunteering and Advocacy:** DEI might inspire us to participate in community initiatives that support marginalized groups or engage in activism aimed at promoting fairness and equality. It might lead us to contribute to organizations that focus on providing resources and opportunities to underrepresented populations.

4. Media and Representation

- **Representation in Media:** DEI is reflected in the media we consume, from movies to news outlets. More diverse representation in movies, TV shows, and books means that we see a wider range of voices, perspectives, and stories that reflect the complexity of human experiences.

- **Cultural Sensitivity:** As we become more aware of DEI, we may become more attuned to how certain groups are represented in the media, and we might question stereotypes or problematic portrayals that reinforce inequality.

5. Personal Growth and Education

- **Learning about Diversity and Bias:** Engaging with DEI issues encourages personal growth, such as learning about other cultures, histories, and experiences. It can help us recognize and address our own biases, leading to more empathetic and respectful interactions.

- **Seeking Diverse Perspectives:** In our education or professional development, DEI encourages us to seek out diverse voices and viewpoints. Whether reading books by authors from different backgrounds or engaging in conversations with people from other cultures, we can deepen our understanding of the world.

6. Challenges and Opportunities

- **Confronting Bias:** In everyday life, we might encounter situations where unconscious biases come into play, either on our part or others'. DEI encourages us to recognize these biases and work to mitigate their effects, whether in personal interactions or in societal systems.

- **Creating Change:** Being mindful of DEI can empower us to take action in our own circles. We might speak out against injustice, advocate for more inclusive practices, or create spaces where people from all walks of life can thrive.

7. Impact on Mental Health and Well-being

- **Belonging and Support:** Inclusion fosters a sense of belonging, which is essential for mental health and well-being. Feeling like we're valued and that our voices matter can have a positive impact on our self-esteem and overall emotional health.

- **Addressing Inequality:** When we witness or experience inequity, it can lead to stress and frustration. DEI initiatives work to address these inequalities, which can, in turn, reduce anxiety and improve the quality of life for individuals who have historically been marginalized.

Conclusion:

DEI in our personal lives doesn't just influence how we interact with others but also affects the way we see ourselves and our role in society. By embracing diversity, equity, and inclusion, we contribute to building a more just and harmonious world where people from all backgrounds feel supported and valued. Whether in our relationships, workplaces, communities, or personal growth, DEI plays a role in shaping a more positive and equitable future for all.

Printed in Great Britain
by Amazon